Teaching Children with Special Learning Needs:

A PROBLEM-SOLVING APPROACH

Milton A. Young

JOHN DAY BOOKS IN

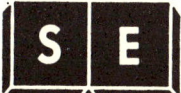

S E

SPECIAL EDUCATION

THE JOHN DAY COMPANY

NEW YORK

TEACHING CHILDREN WITH SPECIAL LEARNING NEEDS:

A Problem-Solving Approach

Dedicated to my wife, Eleanor, and my children, Paul, Susan and Dara, who inspired my work and taught me the real meaning of individual differences, and to all the others whose lives have touched mine and made it more meaningful.

Acknowledgments

Many great men have given me of their wisdom as I passed through college and graduate school, during my teaching career and while I was with the Connecticut State Department of Education. I must mention Dr. Joseph Lavender and Dr. Harold Mahoney. I am grateful to them and to the students at the University of Hartford whose questions sharpened my thinking and whose contributions made this a more useful book. Lastly, this book would not have been completed without those faithful secretaries who spent a great deal of their own time typing and retyping the manuscript.

Contents

Foreword

Dr. Milton Young's approach to *Teaching Children With Special Learning Needs* is a thoughtful, provocative and practical approach to a tremendously complex question, yet one that can be stated so simply: "How can one best help children learn?"

One part of his answer lies in accepting and *utilizing* the fact that children are different. The other part lies in his suggestions that, first, as we move toward planning to meet the individual learning needs of each child, we emphasize a problem-solving technique; second, that as teachers we understand the continuum of problem-solving teaching within the sequence of on-going evaluation, goal-setting and task development.

His main contribution lies in the fact that at this point in time when the concept of diagnostic teaching is being reflected in the development of modern teacher education programs, he has brought together two parts of the answer to the original questions in a compact presentation of philosophy and practice unfettered by continual quotations and references to "the literature." He challenges current concepts of "labeling" children and suggests an alternative procedure.

Teaching Children With Special Learning Needs helps set a new direction to the field in general and to special education in particular. Many teachers will fined it useful for its theory as well as a practical day-to-day tool.

HAROLD J. MAHONEY
Director, Division of Instruction
Connecticut State Department of Education
Hartford, Connecticut

Introduction

The specific purposes of this book are to emphasize the individual differences between children, encourage problem-solving or diagnostic teaching, and give the teacher some assistance in working with children who have difficulties which interfere with their learning. It is not, however, an exhaustive treatise of specific research or an analysis of the thousands of related articles that have appeared in the literature. It suggests a deductive method, followed by creative solutions. It is hoped that the teacher can be helped to see the continuum of problem-solving teaching, within the sequence of ongoing evaluation, goal setting, and task development.

The teacher is the adult model, and children frequently learn by emulation. The teacher who is secure, happy, accepting, interested, and optimistic conveys these feelings to the students, and thus provides the basic ingredients for creating a positive and stimulating learning environment. Any individual who does not possess and cannot cultivate these characteristics should leave teaching.

Good teaching is the ability to keep the child's imagination alive, enabling him to gain insight and skill and helping him to understand the world he lives in. These characteristics are essential to the child's learning to cope with our changing world. On the other hand, poor teaching—narrow, punishing, restrictive, standardized fact-giving—leaves in its wake hostility, ignorance, misunderstanding, conflict, stagnation, negativism, and hopelessness.

Children who are successful in the tasks assigned by the teacher do not present the teacher with a problem (although this approach may also help them). If a child fails in the task he is asked to perform (i.e., if he has a learning problem), the teacher is asked to be creative in his solution of the problem (see Figure I). He must analyze the goals, the task, and his methods, and he may then try a number of solutions to assist the child. The problem and its cause may be very simple, so that the teacher can modify his techniques to overcome it; or it may be complex, requiring considerable ingenuity, imaginative adaptation, and assistance from various specialists. He may try a number of ideas until he discovers those that are helpful. This process is a continuous one. One might ask how the daily goals are determined. The teacher should constantly challenge the child by staying just "one half-step" ahead in each area, always ready to provide help if he begins to falter. In addition to suggesting a method, this book can help him by offering additional techniques when he has exhausted those he can think of himself.

The book makes another point, that labeling a child "mentally retarded," "brain injured," or "socially maladjusted" does not necessarily suggest how the teacher can help him. Labeling has frequently been used as an excuse for failure to teach the child. In each case, a teacher must provide a suitable educational program by himself or with outside assistance. Unfortunately, many teachers do not approach teaching as a problem-solving situation, but have set expectancy for their students. Many children are doomed to failure by a never-ending conflict with the school when they deviate from what is *assumed* to be the normal pattern. Those children who are selected for "special education" fre-

Figure I

A PROBLEM-SOLVING TEACHING APPROACH FOR CHILDREN WHO HAVE LEARNING DIFFICULTIES

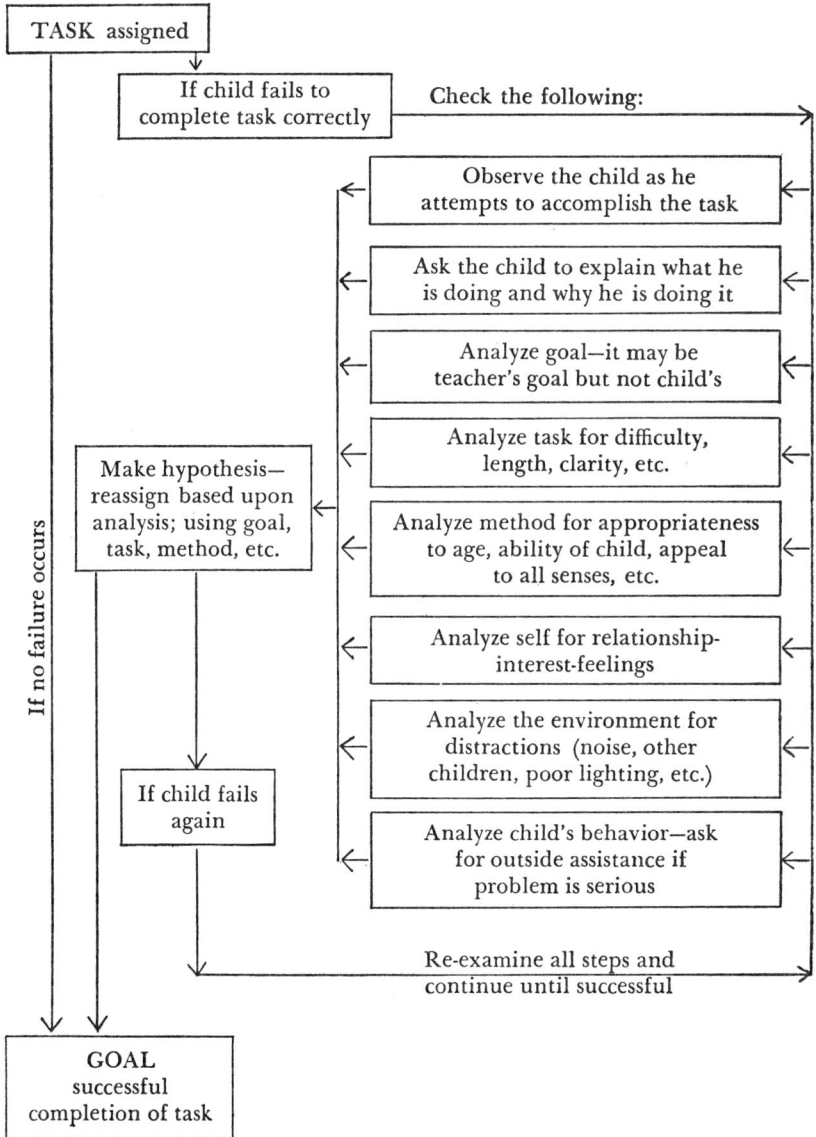

TASK assigned

If child fails to complete task correctly

Check the following:

Observe the child as he attempts to accomplish the task

Ask the child to explain what he is doing and why he is doing it

Analyze goal—it may be teacher's goal but not child's

Analyze task for difficulty, length, clarity, etc.

Make hypothesis—reassign based upon analysis; using goal, task, method, etc.

Analyze method for appropriateness to age, ability of child, appeal to all senses, etc.

Analyze self for relationship-interest-feelings

Analyze the environment for distractions (noise, other children, poor lighting, etc.)

If child fails again

Analyze child's behavior—ask for outside assistance if problem is serious

Re-examine all steps and continue until successful

If no failure occurs

GOAL
successful completion of task

quently suffer the fate of a remorseless negative attitude on the part of everyone in their environment. They are made to feel that they have somehow failed their parents and teachers and are therefore worth less than the others. Some children with learning difficulties are made into lifelong failures because the school is unable to adapt to their problems. In spite of its professed philosophy, it is unable to plan a program which deals with individual differences. The child with a school problem is actually a neglected resource in our nation.

In order for the teacher to be able to utilize his best skills and creativity to teach all children, including those children who have problems, he must have a clear concept of *the knowledge he must possess, the skills that must be mastered, and the resources he can call upon.*

Teachers who are skeptical about the problem-solving approach, or who feel that they do not have the time to think of and plan for each child as an individual, are asked to take one small step at a time, work with one child for a short period of time. As a teacher becomes more comfortable with this method, he can broaden its use. Another possibility is to find another teacher who is willing to try this method, so that the two teachers can work as a team, and each can have someone with whom to discuss his problems. *The teacher has a responsibility for each child who fails to learn in school.*

When a child exhibits a behavior pattern which interferes with learning, he presents a problem which the teacher must solve in a creative manner, not a cause for punishment, failure, or blame. If this book enables the teacher to utilize his creative ability and become a better, more able teacher so that he can prevent children from becoming failures, it will have accomplished its purpose.

M.A.Y.

TEACHING CHILDREN WITH SPECIAL
LEARNING NEEDS:

A Problem-Solving Approach

CHAPTER 1

The School

The Role of the School

The goals of education as stated during recent White House Conferences usually include one for which our country is particularly noted. During the last fifty years we have developed a concept which emphasizes our responsibility for the provision of opportunities for each individual for the fullest development of his own unique talents and skills, limited only by the extent to which he is willing to work toward his development and our own ability to help him. In spite of the tremendous gains in the provision of educational programs for an increasing number of children, in reality the notion of equal educational opportunities for all is a myth. The school frequently appears to be engaged in a battle with the children, often dooming to failure those who deviate from what is assumed to be the normal pattern or those who do not learn well under the existing system. Children with problems which interfere with their learning the tasks set forth by the schools are all too frequently damaged in the educational process.

Providing for Each Child's Needs

The ability of a child to function as a human being in every area is related to the extent to which his basic human needs have been and are being met. In evolving a school program for each youngster, certain general needs of the child need to be considered, no matter what his ability or development. Each child needs to be loved, to feel wanted, to feel that his efforts are appreciated, and to be accepted as he is. He needs to see the world around him as dependable, and people and things as trustworthy. He must have a sense of self-identity so that he knows who he is and what his role is; a sense of accomplishment so that he feels that he is worthwhile and that he can complete the tasks that he attempts. His environment must provide him with a feeling of freedom to try new things and to use his imagination and creativity, and a real choice concerning what he can do, which leads him to a sense of autonomy and individuality.

Problems Caused by the Growth of the Population

The creation of a school system designed to meet the ever-increasing needs of large numbers of children has been undertaken by the people of the United States. This has required the recruitment and training of a vast number of teachers and administrators. Hundreds of thousands of schools have had to be constructed and equipped to house the expanding school-age population. Vast resources of industry have had to be developed in order to produce the teaching materials needed for schoolchildren. This includes the development and production of books as well as laboratory equipment, audio-visual aids, and furniture. Although progress has been made in the development of school facilities, it is still abundantly clear that the percentage of the national wealth that is being spent for educational purposes is much too small. Until the time that a greater share of available funds is appropriated for educational purposes, it will be almost impossible to meet the expanding needs of our children, not to mention improving programs for those in school now.

Children Who Are Not Quick, Facile and Verbal

In the United States, the facts that education is seen as universal and that school attendance is compulsory have created tremendously difficult problems for our children. Tracing the historical development of schools, we see that prior to the concept of compulsory education and industrialization, there was no disgrace when an individual could not perform well in the tasks required by school. Children were not expected to learn to read or write. Most people lived in small communities and were evaluated on the basis of factors other than those which we presently hold to be important. Since most of the population was still illiterate, there was no stigma attached to this state of affairs. The problem that affected only a small number of children a hundred years ago has become one of major proportions today.

The school obviously plays an extremely important role in the community's view of the children attending it and perhaps an even more important role in the child's self-concept, particularly in relation to how well he does the tasks assigned to him in school. As a matter of fact, children who have learning problems or who are not quick, facile and verbal are looked down upon not only by the general community but too often by their own parents. Since the school usually reflects the attitudes of the community, teachers frequently adopt these same attitudes toward children. For the first time in history, since schools are now both universal and compulsory, failure in school or fear of failure has become an important factor in the everyday life of our community. It is worth noting that today our concern for "dropouts" is due to our acceptance of the idea that high school graduation is essential for success and that college training has assumed greater importance.

Even fairly recently, children were able to escape attending school if they were in difficulty or if the school considered them unteachable. When there was a need for child labor, some children were able to leave school by using work as an excuse. Truant officers were not so persistent in tracking down youngsters who left school before compulsory school age.

However, school authorities have too frequently been unable or unwilling to face the fact that they have a different population from the one that was in attendance as recently as thirty years ago. In many cases, they still refuse to acknowledge the fact that there are some children who are not successful in schools as they exist today because they need a program different from the one that is presently offered. Teachers enjoy children who are quick and facile in the tasks they assign and frequently do not adapt their teaching to those who learn more slowly or differently, sometimes because they do not know what to do and often because they are not permitted to do so. Fear of failing in school, and thus being humiliated in the process, has become a tragic experience for a large number of American children and has sometimes led to catastrophic results. The emphasis on science caused by Sputnik has increased the competition and further humiliated those who fail to achieve high grades. In Japan, the admissions competition is actually fiercer than it is in the United States. It begins with five-year-olds, who must learn to count from twenty backward before they are permitted to enter kindergarten. It is reported that suicides there have increased among teenagers who fail to qualify for senior high or college entrance. We obviously need to raise serious questions about the way our schools are structured today and the programs that they conduct, no matter how painful or uncomfortable it is for us to do so.

One of the more serious problems, then, is that, in attempting to respond to one of the major reasons for establishing schools and making attendance compulsory (i.e., teaching the skills of reading, writing and arithmetic so that these are used functionally by adults), coercive, rigid techniques are used, which frequently cause children to hate these areas. Almost all children fear the ridicule of their teachers, and many strive to achieve on a high level, not because they see it as important or are genuinely interested, but because they fear letting their parents and teachers down. Conformity becomes a habit, and children learn to fear trying new things. Taking tests becomes a painful, fearful experience for most children and adults.

In all probability, a good deal of the resentment against schools indicated by the parents' unwillingness to support increased costs for education stems from their own difficulties as students. We could probably even make a further statement with some assurance: many schools appear to cause fear and failure and thereby generate a resentful and hostile student body, thus actually lending themselves to the development of serious learning and behavior problems.

Any concept of equality would recognize that children are significantly different from one another in the ways they learn, how fast they learn, and in their experiences and interests. Equal education means treating them according to their talents and their preferences rather than giving each of them the same program. Scheduling approximately the same program for each child is *actually depriving many children of their rights and is, in effect, unequal education.*

It appears that our efforts to give equal education to each child in our democracy are applied so equally to all children that we disregard individual differences. Thus we reward only those who can learn through the methods and techniques we use. In a real sense, we discriminate against those children who do not follow the predetermined patterns, those who are unable or unwilling to learn by being exposed to the present educational program.

Some time ago Arthur Johnson expressed this idea:

In the past I always accepted the occasional trouble-maker as an inescapable headache for the school. I now know that the school was frequently an even greater headache for that child. For as I better understand the attitudes which underlie anti-social behavior, I see that they often hinge on little things for which the school alone was at fault.

It is so easy to dodge embarrassing issues by treating the problem boy as a discipline case, waiving all personal responsibility by turning him over to the social worker and the courts. These are too often so concerned with opinions of other and untrained observers that they have neither time nor opportunity to study the boy, his personal problems, the real causes for his sorry plight. Altogether too many youngsters are being *judged* bad and, in their youth and pliability, in fact are being *made* bad.[1]

Individual Planning as the Goal

In order to teach democratic values, i.e., to inculcate a positive attitude toward thinking, freedom, and respect for individual differences, we must see to it that teachers provide children with experiences in terms of their own needs, interests and problems. The teacher must provide a stimulating environment and help motivate youngsters so that they have a wide variety of possible interests. Lists of facts and skills in the curriculum should be used only to make certain that teachers do not overlook great bodies of material rather than to force children through minutiae. In planning the children's experiences, consideration must be given to the specific needs that each child has at the present time and those he will have in the future. The teacher must plan her program so that it considers the way in which a youngster learns, his experiences and the level of his skills.

[1] Arthur C. Johnson, Jr., "Our Schools Make Criminals," *Journal of Criminal Law and Criminology*, XXXIII, No. 4 (Nov.–Dec., 1942), pp. 310–12 (reprinted by special permission from the *Journal of Criminal Law and Criminology* (Northwestern University School of Law).

Florence Stratemeyer[2] discusses "persistent life situations" as the basis for achieving the objectives of the school. She states that a curriculum must be based on situations which are evolved by analyzing the daily lives of many individuals and must be built on the knowledge of the learner and utilize the principles of the learning process. It must provide the learner with the key to relating to himself and society. The utilization of the "persistent life situations" approach makes new demands on teachers and schools, since the achievement of any of the goals depends in great measure both on the teachers and on the school conditions which interact with their teaching.

[2] Florence B. Stratemeyer and others, *Developing a Curriculum for Modern Living* (New York, Bureau of Publications, Teachers College, Columbia University, 1957).

CHAPTER 2

The Classroom as a Positive Environment*

The Teacher's Relationship with His Pupils

We are all constantly learning and, in a broad sense, being educated. We learn as we receive new impressions, react to new ideas, relate to new acquaintances, think new thoughts, solve new problems or create new things. In some instances, however, the learning may not help the individual to progress; it may be negative and even depress him to a lower level of function. Just as a flower needs good soil, nutrition and loving care in order to grow and thrive, so children require a stimulating environment and gentle but knowledgeable assistance to mature into functioning adults with a high level of skill and ability. A negative environment can cause the flower to stop growing, distort or twist its shape and, under some conditions, cause it to wither and die. Schools play an essential role in the development of young children, and the teacher is the key to the effectiveness of the educa-

---

* In other sections of this book, we will discuss in some detail factors which can cause problems that interfere with learning. It is obvious that we cannot isolate the classroom environment from the factors that influence it from the outside. However, in the interest of clarity, we will attempt to describe here a wholesome, spontaneous, stimulating learning environment which in itself prevents problems.

tional program. The teacher, through his ability to create a positive and stimulating classroom environment, can enable the child to grow and to develop his own unique talents and skills.

We know that a crucial relationship for each child in school is the one with his teacher. The teacher can function in such a way that he acts in a supportive, stimulating role with the child as he learns. One of the most important problems that the teacher faces is the complexity and multiplicity of his roles and the factors that affect what he does in the classroom. These include his own self-concept, his relationship with the children in his class and the concept of him held by his pupils, by parents, school administrators and society.

The teacher must first accept himself as a worthwhile individual before he can accept children as they are and create an atmosphere of security in the classroom. If the teacher feels superior or inadequate (two sides of the same coin), these feelings are conveyed to the children and prohibit the development of a wholesome emotional climate in the classroom. In such a situation, children feel strange, unaccepted and rebellious.

Sometimes the superiority feelings of the teacher take on subtle forms. Some teachers may prefer children who act just as they do, may try to mold others to their own image of themselves. These teachers often fail to understand the wide differences among people that are acceptable in our pluralistic society and the concept that different values and ideas contribute to the welfare of everyone. Other teachers may feel that they have become teachers by accident, without having chosen this profession. Children may, perhaps unconsciously, resent such a teacher and thus create additional problems by sensing basic feelings about his position. A teacher who feels that he is superior, who has serious feelings of insecurity, or who resents the fact that he is teaching cannot provide a wholesome, energetic classroom environment.

He must seek to examine and eliminate these attitudes and overcome his feelings (with help if necessary) , or else leave teaching.

The feelings teachers have about individual students are extremely important. Children tend to perform in the manner teachers expect them to and, as a corollary, teachers tend to find in children the behavior they expect to find. This has been referred to as a "self-fulfilling prophecy." These statements should give most teachers reason to pause and consider their feelings about children and the actions which communicate these feelings.

Placing a child in a particular group indicates what the teacher expects of him. Consider what the consequences of grouping for reading in first grade can be. As a result of his scores on a reading test, Billy is placed in a group called the "Bluejays." In spite of calling the groups by such names to camouflage them, Billy soon discovers that he is in the slowest reading group. He finds that the teacher does not demand too much from him and overlooks mistakes which he is really capable of correcting. He accepts being slow as a fact. He may continue to learn slowly and he considers himself less able than those in the groups above him. His feelings about his abilities become part of his behavior. In this way we have perpetrated one of the greatest crimes committed by education. Basing our actions upon a test which is really of little significance, we have developed a child who has negative feelings about himself and his ability to learn and who now tests and performs as a child with problems in learning.

It appears self-evident that a teacher who gives a test when he knows that half the children will fail is failing only himself. If he knows that they will not pass the test, what has he gained by proving it? He has only punished the children. The approach of the teacher must be just the opposite. He must want and work toward having each student achieve success. His job is not to identify the failures, criticize the mistakes, sort out the slow students or label the children to disguise the fact that he failed to teach them. The teacher must look at his students and believe that each has dignity and can make a contribution to society. Even when a child presents him with serious problems, when he is inattentive, aggressive, dirty, and cannot get along, it is the duty of the teacher to find a way to reach him. While he may not be successful with every child, he must do all he can to find their strengths and help develop them. While tests can help find flaws in children's skills or lack of knowledge, the teacher who feels responsible can provide the bridge to experiences that will motivate the child to grow and improve.

Classroom Environment

Teachers must be particularly aware of the environment they create in their classrooms. Children bring many different backgrounds and experiences with them. Their attitudes, motivation, development and readiness are quite varied. There are a number of basic feelings and significant considerations about himself and the children that the teacher must be mindful of as he plans his work with them. These include:

1. A FEELING OF BEING ACCEPTED. Every child needs a feeling of being accepted for what he is and for the contribution he can make to the lives of others. There are a number of "tricks of the trade" that experienced teachers use to make it abundantly clear that each child in the class is important. Some children have already heard some things about their new teacher, others have had contact during previous years. However, a positive relationship, established during the very first contacts of the new year, will create an important link

to future behavior. Some examples are knowing and using children's names, taking time to talk to each child, and being interested in what the children say. The teacher who creates a positive environment is one who:

a. Remembers special events, birthdays
b. Takes a personal interest in each child
c. Finds personal things to say
d. Picks up the child's special interests
e. Shares the fun with the children
f. Discusses the problems and listens to their points of view

It is easy to teach likable children; however, some children are difficult to like. There may be one who is not always clean, whose hair is not combed; one who does not appear to listen to you, who refuses to do as he is asked; one who seems to be lazy, and others. Teachers who really care about children see their profession as one that is dedicated to *helping* children learn. They include as part of their task an attempt to solve the problems that present themselves as barriers to learning. The lazy teacher gives up very quickly; the authoritative teacher refuses to be concerned about the child who does not follow orders; the subject-matter-oriented teacher is interested only in those who learn what he teaches, the others being dismissed as failures, retarded or lazy. Even the good teacher frequently neglects a child because he does not fit into the pattern of what he thinks ought to go on in the classroom.

The task of the teacher is to teach each child. The ones who learn easily hardly need help at all. Sometimes a teacher dislikes a child and does not know why. This may be because the child has different standards from his own. In other instances, the child reminds him of a person he dislikes or some trait within himself that he is trying to hide. In any event, the teacher who feels that *he* cannot be the cause of the problem is not being fair to the child. Perhaps only careful analysis of his feelings, or outside help, such as a conference with a psychiatrist, psychologist or a social worker, will bring the truth out into the open. It takes a great deal of courage to ask for someone to help look at one's own problems and motives.

It is the teacher's responsibility to build a positive, constructive relationship with each child. The teacher must interact to help the child learn. This does not mean that an accepting attitude is a permissive, unstructured environment or lack of discipline. Children need to know the limits, and they depend on the teacher to guide them in their behavior. Since no one is right all the time, conflicts do occur, and the teacher who is firm but warm does the most toward creating an environment in which children can be free to learn.

2. SUCCESS LEADS TO SUCCESS. All children must feel that they are succeeding in what they are doing. There must be a feeling of accomplishment. Each child perceives his environment in terms of his feelings about himself. If he has met with mistrust, disinterest, rejection or harassment, and has been treated as if he were stupid, a failure, of low ability or different, he sees the world as a hostile place, and his attempts to cope with it are reflected in his actions. The child's image of himself is a major factor in determining his success as a learner.

The teacher who helps a child build a positive image of himself, and expects accomplishment, is making the child feel that he is unique and worthwhile, and this encourages him to do his best in his own way.

The public is always very excited about the children who are the most successful, at the top of the class, forgetting that *most* children are not. When a child is doing his best, he must be made to feel he is worthwhile. We often say such things as, "Let's see who can finish *first*" and "Who has the *neatest* paper?" These statements often destroy the initiative of the child who cannot do better than everyone else. We must remember that most parents send their children to school to learn, not to be best at everything they do. We must accept the fact that children learn in many different ways and become proficient at a wide variety of skills. Some pick up the skills by using books; others learn through discussions; while still others learn best when involved in practical situations. The objective is to see that each child continues to grow and is stimulated to continue to learn and explore.

3. CHILDREN LEARN BEST WHEN THEY PARTICIPATE. A child needs to feel part of the group. This can be accomplished by providing him with an opportunity to participate in an active manner, so that he can *experience* learning instead of sitting passively and permitting it to filter in. If we want to teach each child to think for himself, we must create experiences and situations wherein he must think in order to be successful. The teacher who constantly gives directions leaves little for the child to decide or work through. Too often, a child's creative, challenging questions will be denied by the authoritarian teacher. Children frequently do not feel that they are participating with their group, but that they are simply responding to the teacher as individuals.

A child needs to be successful in his experiences in group situations. He develops a concept of himself in relation to these early experiences. If he fails rather consistently, he develops a sense of defeat, of doubt. This may keep him from participating further or cause him to be more concerned with his self-image than with the activities of the group, resulting in his becoming a clown or a bully. The skilled teacher develops experiences which help the group accept differences among its members. Being able to work with others is a skill that can frequently spell the difference between success and failure as an adult.

The teacher must plan carefully for group participation experiences. William Hollister suggests some guidelines:

> Each person comes to (a class) as an individual. He has his own ideas, his own feelings, his own reasons for being there. And, unless we consciously utilize that individuality, he may leave at the end of the session just as he came—a little richer in facts and ideas, perhaps, but still without the deeper emotional understandings and social experiences basic to personal growth.
>
> Some of these deeper emotional understandings can develop if the individual has a chance to give of himself in a group setting. The separate individuals can join together, thinking and feeling more and more as one, as they work toward common goals. Together, you and your group can build a climate where every member accepts every other member, where each person's contribution is considered significant.
>
> This is the group experience, which is hard to describe because so much of it lies in the realm of feelings. Once you have experienced it, you can feel the difference—a warm, safe, secure climate which encourages a deeper sharing and often brings about important attitude changes.
>
> Whether or not the [class achieves] this group experience depends to a considerable extent on you, their [teacher]. There's no blueprint for bringing it about. It depends on such intangible things as your manner, the tone of your voice, and the way you handle your position of leadership. Most of all it depends on your ability to communicate your conviction that all people are important [including children]. . . .
>
> Participation is, of course, the heart of the group experience. Helping individuals to participate is a major part of your role as (teacher).[3]

[3] William G. Hollister, *Suggested Techniques for Teaching Group Discussions*. Department of Mental Health, National Institute of Health, in Gladys Gardner Jenkins, ed., *Helping Children Reach Their Potential*. Scott, Forsman & Co., Chicago, 1961.

The following suggestions may serve as group work guides:

a. Meet the group's dependency needs. This requires that the group do something it wants to do rather quickly to prove it can be successful.
b. Provide early group success.
c. Share leadership with the group. Children can contribute leadership acts if they feel safe to do so. Plan to have each child have a role.
d. Let the group plan for itself, limiting its planning only when absolutely necessary, not to avoid mistakes which they should be able to make and correct but in regard to safety or general school policy.
e. Help the group evaluate what it has done. This may occur during the group meeting as well as afterwards.

The classroom teacher encourages each child to utilize his own talent, interest and ability to make his contribution to the class. Each student feels that he is different, and these differences make him a key member in the class.

All children must learn to communicate with each other. This ability to communicate is frequently undeveloped. Even teachers develop serious communication problems with the children. Careful plans to open communications is an obvious need in the classroom.

Some children do not easily establish rapport and participate in the class or other smaller groups. There are many reasons for this behavior and the teacher may be able to determine what they are by careful observation and a friendly relationship. Misunderstandings, prejudices, ignorance, and other characteristics of the group may contribute to the isolation of some individuals. Role playing, socio-drama (acting out troublesome situations) and other techniques may be used to overcome such problems.

4. ACCEPTANCE OF EACH CHILD'S FEELINGS. The teacher must create an atmosphere in which children feel that they can express themselves and their feelings. This includes the feelings which are contrary to the group, as well as new and creative feelings which may be different. How a child expresses his feelings is a clue to his personality. The child who is open, unafraid and curious is easy to work with and is usually anxious to learn. The child who expresses excessive anger, hostility, etc., over a period of time needs our help in learning how to cope with these feelings. The teacher who forces a child to deny his emotions may also be causing him to develop problems which will interfere with his learning. Statements like "You aren't really afraid" and "It isn't like you to get so nervous" create an atmosphere which represses the expression of real feelings by the children. "Many people become fearful in new situations" and "I'm nervous, too" are comments designed to encourage expression of feelings. There is a difference between permitting a child to express his feelings and accepting his behavior, so that we may accept his feelings and reject his behavior as interfering with others. When the teacher has created an atmosphere where every child's feelings are accepted, there is less likelihood that there will be outbursts or withdrawal.

Those who work with children and other adults and attempt to listen and communicate realize the difficulties this entails. Since we all see the world in terms of our own experiences and our interpretation of them, we can never really understand every nuance of what another person is attempting to convey. Communications are better when they are kept open and where there is mutual trust. Actually, communication includes not only words, spoken or written; nonverbal behavior such as a smile, a pat on the back, a hug, etc., often expresses feelings better than words. Children who have problems which interfere with their learning are likely to be especially sensitive to the feelings communicated to them by the teacher. The teacher who becomes angry because of a child's slowness or inability to understand quickly closes the communication channels.

The child who exhibits behavior that stands out from the rest of the children usually needs the attention of the teacher and perhaps of others. The teacher who is sensitive to the child's feelings also notices changes in his performance. When a quiet child suddenly lashes out, or a happy child becomes unusually sad, the teacher should make an effort to determine the basis for the change.

Sometimes, evidence conveying the feelings of children is exposed during informal activities. The teacher may gain insights during an unassigned time, during lunch or after school, outside on the playground, through role playing, the child's art production, or what he writes about. When we are concerned with each child and his unique pattern and his own means of expression, we become aware of his abilities and needs, and of what he can give. As we study the child, we bring our skill and understanding to help reach him and guide him so he can be a positive part of the world around him.

5. LEARNING INDEPENDENCE. The ability to function independently is an essential ingredient in learning to cope with one's environment. An accepting teacher who understands the needs of children creates a wholesome situation which encourages self-reliance and independence. While most children need help to determine the best direction to take in a number of situations, they must also have the freedom to make their own decisions. Accepting the teacher as an adult who will guide only when necessary gives the child an opportunity and the confidence to learn independence and self-direction.

If the teacher insists that all wrongs must be punished and

regulations strictly enforced, he is providing the children with as real a cell as if they were in prison. As a matter of fact, if a child is trained in the importance of following *every* rule, he will not be able to adjust where these regulatons do not apply or when they are changed. He will be attracted to the authoritarian leader who has rules for all types of behavior and who arises in our country and the world from time to time.

Children take over standards set by parents and their teachers, and these control their behavior even when the controlling agents are not present. The teacher should attempt to set guidelines for behavior and provide opportunities for children to develop and use self-control. In some instances, however, the teacher's and the child's standards may be different, at which point communication breaks down. When such a situation occurs and blocks the child's performance in the classroom, the teacher should attempt to discover the cause of the problem. A discussion of difference in values and expectancies appears in a later chapter. Self-discipline and independent behavior are among the main goals of the school, and their evolvement requires a consideration of all the positive elements that make for a real learning environment.

The feelings of the teacher and those of the child—the child's individuality, his need to belong, to succeed, to be accepted, his role as a group member, what he brings to the class in terms of values and attitude, etc.—all these factors determine the degree of independent behavior a child can be helped to attain. The assumption of responsibility by the schools for their role in achieving these goals places the burden of improved programs directly on them.

In short, if the teacher really wants to know his pupils, to understand them, to help them recognize their strengths, weaknesses and purposes, and to have faith in their potential, he will improve his ability to help them realize it.

Kimball Wiles[4] summarizes the teacher's contributions to the student's feelings of acceptance as follows:

a. *Calling by name:* Each of us likes the recognition that comes from having his first name used. Calling youngsters by their first names creates a situation which tells each child that the teacher is close to him. The use of first names is symbolic and revealing of the teacher's feelings.

b. *Responding to ideas:* Even attentive listening is not enough. Since the most effective learning occurs through the interaction of ideas, teaching is made most meaningful through thoughtful acceptance of and response to pupil ideas.

c. *Taking questions seriously:* Children sometimes ask naive questions. However, they are very important to the child who asks them. Naturally, any question seems simple to a person who already knows the answer. Respecting the other person and working with him in a way that helps him grow require an acceptance of his questions as being noteworthy of consideration.

d. *Avoiding ridicule and sarcasm:* Respect for human personality is taught by example. If a teacher ridicules individual students, he makes clear to all that he does not respect the personalities of children. But by showing proper respect for each child, he increases the chance that the boys and girls with whom he works will respect each other.

e. *Avoiding action that embarrasses:* Embarrassing a pupil splits the group into two camps. All the members feel that they must take sides. They are forced either to defend the injured person or to declare their allegiance to the teacher. Such issues can be avoided if the teacher

4 Kimball Wiles, *Teaching for Better Schools* (Englewood Cliffs, N.J., Prentice-Hall, Inc.), pp. 58–59, 1959.

takes the misbehaving youngster aside and talks over with him the effect of his behavior on the group.

f. *Encouraging friendliness:* By complimenting pupils on their acts of friendliness, friendliness in the group is increased.

g. *Welcoming children:* Welcoming new children into the group makes it clear that friendliness and belonging are essential qualities of that group. As a teacher plans with the members of his class how they can make new members feel at home, he shows that all people belong and are wanted. He assures the newcomers that they are welcome, and at the same time he increases the security and acceptance of the other children.

h. *Letting absentees know that they were missed:* When absentees know that they have been missed, they feel that they are making a contribution to the group. But when they return unnoticed, they gain the impression that no one cares whether they are part of the group or not.

i. *Permitting students to choose their own seats:* If the teacher assigns seats arbitrarily, he makes it clear that the room is really his room and that the students are simply doing his bidding. But if he allows students to sit with their friends, he shows that he is working with them in a situation in which friendship is valued and respected. By separating friends, he makes clear that friendship is not a quality that he values in the classroom. The problem of what to do about cliques can be effectively handled after the children have come to recognize friendship as a positive value. Then the problem can be tackled by all the members of the group. The solution worked out by this method will be far more satisfactory than when the teacher sets out to destroy the cliques by seating youngsters away from the people with whom they would prefer to sit.

j. *Having the class work in small groups toward common goals:* As pupils have an opportunity to work closely together in small groups, friendships and a sense of belonging increase, especially if the children are encouraged to carry out their own ideas.

k. *Stressing common qualities while accepting differences:* By suggesting that there are some common interests, a teacher helps children feel secure in accepting differences. Group unity is built around common purposes, interests and beliefs.

l. *Refraining from punishing children by sending them from the room:* Sending a youngster from the room is unfortunate for the teacher and the child, and should be avoided. It decreases the child's self-respect and isolates him from the group. The effects of such isolation are particularly harmful to children who are already having difficulty getting along with others. Such action represents the failure of the teacher—not the child.

Flexibility as the Key to Grouping

Grouping is a tool of the teacher, not a straightjacket imposed on the teacher and his class. If the teacher is really interested in each child, he uses the group as an aid to learning. Unfortunately, some grouping begins before the teacher ever sees the children. Homogeneous, or ability, grouping of children has been and still is a convenient device for administering overcrowded schools. It is used to convince some parents that their children are getting a superior education. Although a great deal has been written about various techniques for grouping, comparing homogeneous and heterogeneous groups, there is as much evidence favoring one as the other. The most negative and damaging consequence of so-called homogeneous grouping is the frequent assumption that all the children in a particular group are the same. This results in the teacher's trying to teach all the children in the group the same things in the same way. Actually, no group can be homogeneous except for a short period of time and in a rather narrow area of skill. As educators achieve greater awareness of the multiple dimensions of each child, they begin to realize that any attempt at a homogeneous, fixed grouping pattern is futile.

Probably a number of teachers use groups to the detriment of the children. Some of the harm results from comments such as, "Try harder, maybe you'll get up into the next group" (some never make it) ; "If you don't behave or do your work I will put you in 'that' group"; "You can't do that work, your group is not up to it," or "No, you can't learn that now, that's in next year's curriculum." The key to grouping is flexibility and variety of size. *A group should exist for a specific purpose for a short period of time, then it should be disbanded or changed.*

Competing for High Marks as a Cause of Cheating

When teachers or parents stress marks or high scores, children have a greater tendency to cheat. The younger the child, the stronger the tendency is for him to cheat as a means of keeping from failing. Children must have a large number of successful experiences before they begin to learn to accept failure or second best. A great deal of harm can be caused when competition is stressed too early in a child's life. In some cases, children obtain rather extreme feelings about competition, and psychological problems result. When we attempt to teach the child to face the competition of the real world, we must do so very carefully, to prevent a point of view that is distorted. In any event, the skilled teacher can use competition constructively by first preparing the children with a large number of successes and then by providing a carefully balanced program so that all children have a chance to do well.

Pressure as a Cause of Problems

Schools tend to pressure children to the point that many of them become very anxious and some develop serious emotional problems. Tests, quizzes, homework, emphasis on high grades and strict requirements all have the effect of making students extremely tense. While some children have the problem of being separated from a highly overprotective mother, more of them are under constant self-pressure to please their parents by obtaining high marks and good grades.

Frequently, parents pressure children and blame the schools for not making the child work harder. Since parents are emotionally involved with their children and often lack an understanding of how children learn, when they attempt to help them, they soon find themselves in extremely tense and unhappy situations, straining the relationship with their children. The great public cry against the new mathematics program stems partially from the fact that parents do not understand it. This prevents them from determining how well the children are learning.

Teachers also set up specific, narrow programs and requirements which demand that children conform. The problems faced by the child who varies from the pattern pressure most children into conforming to the specific work laid out by the teacher.

Motivation

An essential element of learning is motivation. The key to motivation is usually the child's interest. Since most children seem to have an internal pressure which causes them to attempt to learn new things, teachers who study children to determine what their interests are, and are skillful in encouraging them so that the child becomes involved in the classroom work, need not worry about motivation. Some teachers, however, are unable to cope with children's ideas and frequently cause their high degree of interest to falter.

If a child does not see the importance of what we decide he should learn, he cannot be made to learn it. The *child* determines what he wants to learn, not the teacher. Many children develop behavior characteristics that interfere with their learning because the teacher fails to consider the importance of the child's being interested in what he is trying to learn.

Children succeed because a great many factors have been brought into a positive relationship with each other. Raymond Kuhlen says:

> Achievement is, of course, the result of many factors. It is the product of motivation, of the amount of energy that is thrown into the task at hand, of the health possessed by the subject, of his general emotional and personal and social adjustment, of the conditions of work, of his background skills both with respect to the particular task at hand and more general skills of how to work and think. All of these factors and others not easily identifiable combine to constitute functioning intelligence. Schools and individuals might profitably examine some of these factors with a view to improving in a practical way the capacity to achieve.
>
> Among people of exceptional accomplishment in the arts, sheer talent is only one requisite for success. Along with talent must go a strong drive, physical capacity to stand up under long hours of labor, a stimulating early environment to nurture interest, and the gaining of sufficient emotional satisfactions from the endeavor itself to maintain the motivation essential to further serious applications. Talent alone, without the drive and the physical stamina to capitalize it, does not lead to outstanding achievement.[5]

[5] Raymond G. Kuhlen, *The Psychology of Adolescent Development* (New York: Harper & Brothers, 1952), p. 129.

Using Sound Principles of Learning in the Classroom

Educators concerned with children's learning have the responsibility of formulating the best opportunities for learning. The elements that they have to deal with are time, space, resources and people.

We are concerned not only with *what* is to be learned but also with *how* it is learned. Curriculum guides, lists of objectives, and experiences and goals provide us with what should be learned. Considerable time can be fruitfully spent on the subject of when and in what sequence certain experiences should be presented and certain subject matter taught. New material is being discovered so rapidly that it is almost impossible to keep the teacher up-to-date. The curriculum for each school system must be developed by the teacher in that system and continuously revised. It should serve as a guide for teachers who learn from it just what the community sees as goals for its children. While there is some controversy regarding the type and level of material taught in the school, the question of how to teach for the goals of education represents a maze which is the result of misunderstandings, ignorance, rigidity, poor training, pressure, lack of faith in children, overcrowded classrooms, and many other factors. No subject is more fraught with violent differences of opinion than the question of the best methods and techniques to use in teaching.

The teacher is never a finished product; he is always in training. He must always be alert to new research findings, new programs and new knowledge. Goodwin Watson[6] published a summary list of principles which represent much of what we really know about learning. He says:

[6] Goodwin Watson, "What Do We Know About Learning?" *National Education Association Journal,* March 1963. Reprinted by permission.

Although no scientific "truths" are established beyond the possibility of revision, knowledgeable psychologists generally agree on a number of propositions about learning which are important for education. The educator who bases his program on the propositions below is entitled, therefore, to feel that he is on solid psychological ground and not on shifting sands.

• Behaviors which are rewarded (reinforced) are more likely to recur.

This most fundamental law of learning has been demonstrated in literally thousands of experiments. It seems to hold for every sort of animal from earthworms to highly intelligent adults. The behavior most likely to emerge in any situation is that which the subject found successful or satisfying previously in a similar situation. No other variable affects learning so powerfully. The best-planned learning provides for a steady, cumulative sequence of successful behaviors.

• Reward (reinforcement), to be most effective in learning must follow almost immediately after the desired behavior and be clearly connected with that behavior in the mind of the learner.

The simple word "Right," coming directly after a given response, will have more influence on learning than any big reward which comes much later or which is dimly connected with many responses so that it can't really reinforce any of them. Much of the effectiveness of programed self-instruction lies in the fact that information about success is fed back immediately for each learner response. A total mark on a test the day after it is administered has little or no reinforcement value for the specific answers.

• Sheer repetition without indications of improvement or any kind of reinforcement (reward) is a poor way to attempt to learn.

Practice is not enough. The learner cannot improve by repeated efforts unless he is informed whether or not each effort has been successful.

• Threat and punishment have variable and uncertain effects upon learning: They may make the punished response more likely or less likely to recur; they may set up avoidance tendencies which prevent further learning.

Punishment is not, psychologically, the reverse of reward. It disturbs the relationship of the learner to the situation and the teacher. It does not assist the learner in finding and fixing the correct response.

• Readiness for any new learning is a complex product of interaction among such factors as (a) sufficient physiological and psychological maturity, (b) sense of the importance of the new learning for the learner in his world, (c) mastery of prerequisites providing a fair chance of success, and (d) freedom from discouragement (expectation of failure) or threat (sense of danger).

Conversely, the learner will not be ready to try new responses which are beyond his powers or are seen as valueless or too dangerous.

• Opportunity for fresh, novel, stimulating experience is a kind of reward which is quite effective in conditioning and learning.

Experiments indicate that lower animals (rats, dogs, monkeys) will learn as effectively when they receive rewards of new experience or satisfied curiosity as they will when the rewards gratify physical desires. Similarly, stimulating new insights have been found to be effective as rewards for the learning efforts of human beings.

• The sense of satisfaction which results from achievement is the type of reward (reinforcement) which has the greatest transfer value to other life situations.

Any extrinsic reward—candy, or stars on a chart, or commendation—depends on its dispenser. There is no need to strive if the reward-giver is out of the picture. Also, cheating can sometimes win the extrinsic reward. The internal reward system is always present for the learner, and he sees little gain in fooling himself.

• Learners progress in an area of learning only as far as they need to in order to achieve their purposes. Often they do only well enough to "get by"; with increased motivation, they improve.

Studies of reading speed show that practice alone will not bring improvement; a person may have read books for years at his customary rate, but with new demands and opportunities he may be able to double that rate.

• The most effective effort is put forth by children when they attempt tasks which are not too easy and not too hard—where success seems quite possible but not certain. It is not reasonable to expect a teacher to set an appropriate level of challenge for each pupil in a class; pupils can, however, be helped to set their own goals to bring maximum satisfaction and learning.

• Children are more likely to throw themselves wholeheartedly into any learning project if they themselves have participated in the selection and planning of the project.

Genuine participation (not pretended sharing) increases motivation, adaptability, and speed of learning.

• Excessive direction by the teacher is likely to result in apathetic conformity, defiance, scapegoating, or escape from the whole affair.

Autocratic leadership has been found to increase dependence of members on the leader and to generate resentment (conscious or unconscious) which finds expression in attacks on weaker figures or even in sabotage of the work.

• Overstrict discipline is associated with more conformity anxiety, shyness, and acquiescence in children; greater permissiveness is associated with more initiative and creativity.

In comparisons of children whose parents were most permissive in home discipline with those whose parents were most strict (both groups of parents loving and concerned), the youngsters from permissive homes showed more enterprise, self-confidence, curiosity, and originality.

• Many pupils experience so much criticism, failure, and discouragement in school that their self-confidence, level of aspiration, and sense of worth are damaged.

The pupil who sees himself at his worst in school is likely to place little value on study and to seek his role of importance outside the classroom. He may carry through life a sense of being not good for much. He is likely also to feel resentment toward schools, teachers, and books.

• When children or adults experience too much frustration, their behavior ceases to be integrated, purposeful, and rational. The threshold of what is "too much" varies; it is lowered by previous failures.

Pupils who have had little success and almost continuous failure at school tasks are in no condition to think, to learn, or even to pay attention. They may turn their anger outward against respectable society or inward against themselves.

• Pupils think whenever they encounter an obstacle, difficulty puzzle, or intellectual challenge which interests them. The process of thinking involves designing and testing plausible solutions for the problem as understood by the thinker.

The best way to help pupils form a general concept is to present the concept in numerous and varied specific situations —contrasting experiences with and without the desired concept—and then to encourage precise formulations of the general idea and its application in situations different from those in which the concept was learned.

For example, the concept of democracy might be illustrated not only in national government but also in familiar situations of home, school, church, jobs, clubs, and local affairs. It is best understood when it is contrasted with other power structures such as autocracy, oligarchy, or *laissez faire.*

• The experience of learning by sudden insight into a previously confused or puzzling situation arises when (a) there has been a sufficient background and preparation, (b) attention is given to the relationships operative in the whole situation, (c) the perceptual structure "frees" the key elements to be shifted into new patterns, (d) the task is meaningful and within the range of ability of the subject.

The term "cognitive reorganization" is sometimes applied to this experience. Suddenly the scene changes into one that seems familiar and can be coped with.

• Learning from reading is facilitated more by time spent recalling what has been read than by re-reading.

In one experiment (typical of many), students who spent eighty percent of their learning periods trying to remember what they had read surpassed those who spent only sixty percent of the time on recollection. The students who spent all the time reading and re-reading the assignment made the poorest record.

• Forgetting proceeds rapidly at first—then more and more slowly. Recall shortly after learning reduces the amount forgotten.

Within twenty-four hours after learning something, a large part is forgotten unless efforts are made to prevent forgetting. A thing can be relearned more quickly than it was learned originally, however, and if it is reviewed several times at gradually increasing intervals, it can be retained for some time.

• People remember new information which confirms their previous attitudes better than they remember new information which runs counter to their previous attitudes.

Studies consistently show that individuals who feel strongly on a controversial issue, and who are asked to read presentations of both sides, remember the facts and arguments which support their feelings better than they recall those on the opposite side.

• What is learned is most likely to be available for use if it is learned in a situation much like that in which it is to be used and immediately preceding the time when it is needed. Learning in childhood, then forgetting and later relearning when need arises is not an efficient procedure.

The best time to learn is when the learning can be useful. Motivation is then strongest and forgetting less of a problem. Much that is now taught children might be more effective if taught to responsible adults.

• If there is a discrepancy between the real objectives and the tests used to measure achievement, the latter become the main influence upon choice of subject matter and method. Curriculum and teaching geared to standardized tests and programed learning are likely to concentrate only on learnings which can be easily checked and scored.

• The most rapid mental growth comes during infancy and early childhood; the average child achieves about half of his total mental growth by age five.

In the first two years a normal child transforms the "big, buzzing, blooming confusion" of his first conscious experience to organized perception of familiar faces, spoken words, surroundings, toys, bed, clothing, and foods. He differentiates himself from others, high from low, many from few, approval from disapproval. He lays a foundation for lifelong tendencies toward trust or mistrust, self-acceptance or shame, initiative or passivity; and these vitally condition further growth.

• Not until adolescence do most children develop the sense of time which is required for historical perspective. The so-called facts of history—1492, 1776, and all that—can be learned by children but without any real grasp of what life was like in another period or in a different country. Most instruction in ancient, medieval, and even modern history is no more real to children than are fairy tales.

• Ability to learn increases with age up to adult years. The apparent decline is largely the result of lack of motivation. We can coerce children into school activities; adult education is mostly voluntary. Men and women *can,* if they wish, master new languages, new ideas, and new ways of acting or problem-solving even at sixty and seventy years of age.

Dealing with Individual Difficulties

Each teacher and each child is a unique individual, differing from all others in the way he learns. No two individuals interact in the same way, and no two situations ever occur in exactly the same manner.

If, in addition to all of the complicated learning patterns that ordinarily develop, the conditions are such that an internal or external problem causes any child to have any other difficulties in learning, the teacher must have even greater skill in helping this child.

The child with a learning problem may be one who, for any of a wide variety of reasons, has not had experiences and opportunities similar to those of most children, or he may be one whose pattern of growth and development has been interfered with. The actual cause of the problem may be difficult to find, since the problem that interferes with the child's learning may actually be a complicated combination of behavior and physical problems. But, since the cause may determine the exact course to follow in order to deal with the problem, it must be investigated. In many cases, the effects are of much greater importance than the cause however, since the teacher must work to overcome the effects and may not be able to deal with the cause.

An example might be the process of learning to speak. Most children babble; hearing their own sounds, they repeat them. Later on, they hear words and repeat them. Soon they build up a vocabulary of words, organize them into categories, and use them to learn new things. A child who cannot hear well not only misses the opportunity to learn to speak but all of the learning that comes from using words.

Any such sequence of behavior deprivations will produce a child who has trouble functioning in a classroom situation that is organized for children who have had all of the expected experiences during the period of their growth and development. A teacher who is alert to problems which interfere with learning will usually recognize this child. However, in too many instances he suggests that a child's behavior is his own fault. This child is frequently called lazy, unreasonable, etc., when actually he may be confused and unprepared.

There are children who do not finish their work, are clumsy in their walking, do not appear to pay attention, do not follow directions, etc., who behave in this manner because they are unable to do otherwise. *When a child exhibits a behavior pattern which interferes with learning, he presents a problem that the teacher must solve, in one way or another, not a situation for punishment, failure or blame.*

Elizabeth Freidus[7] suggests that as we look at a child's growth from infancy, we should think of it as an increased widening of relationship between the self and the environment. Each time the senses become aware of a request of something to do, the request is focused upon them and associated with similar information and experience that are relevant, so that the request has some meaning. When the individual feels he understands the meaning, he suggests a response to himself. This response is frequently mentally matched with the request and the possible consequences of action. If this action appears appropriate, it is taken. The child then feeds the perceived consequences back, and attempts to determine if the action was correct. Whether it was correct or not, the new experience is added to his storehouse of information for further reference. If it is incorrect, an-

[7] Elizabeth Freidus, "Methodology for the Classroom Teacher," in *The Special Child in Century 21,* Jerome Hellmuth, ed. (Seattle, The Special Child Publications, 1964) , pp. 303–321.

other solution may be attempted, following the same procedure. If it is correct, no further action may be taken.

A child may have a problem which interferes in any of various aspects of receiving information or giving a response. The reason for his inability or unwillingness to respond or for his giving a response which is in error may be the result of any one of a great *many* causes.

When we are aware of a child who has problems which interfere with learning, we must attempt to help overcome them. We can create an environment in which he feels accepted, help him to perceive the world in a more positive manner, and teach him how to overcome the problems, perhaps by using special techniques or information. As he becomes more competent in the area in which his problems exist, his entire function will probably improve, since he is improving his relationship with his environment.

Since the particular combinations of problems vary from one child to the next, the teacher must have an extensive repertory of techniques and approaches from which to choose. Each experience provides the children with a number of opportunities to learn how to function. The teacher must be skilled in breaking down each activity to its component parts and must understand how each area of growth takes place. He must devise a specific set of activities for a particular set of problems.

CHAPTER 3

Individual Evaluation: The Key to Effective Planning

Comprehensive, Continuous Evaluation

1. THE IMPORTANCE OF EVALUATION. The ability to evaluate children's behavior and performance and convert his own findings and those of others into practical day-to-day activities is an absolutely essential skill for a teacher. A teacher who lacks this skill may be using a preplanned program which bears little relationship to the abilities and needs of his children and which may, in fact, be the cause of many of their problems. A teacher should be constantly gathering and considering evidence which may be indicative of progress toward the achievement of goals, changes in the behavior of children, and problems that prevent learning. Evaluation is an essential and integral part of the process of education. The appraisal of children's functions in school cannot be concerned only with their academic achievements, but must concern itself with their entire behavior spectrum as it influences their progress to the successful accomplishment of the goals set by the school.

The educational activities planned by the teacher should

be determined by the abilities, skills, interests and experiences of the pupils in his room. For a teacher to begin teaching with preconceived, canned programs is like an architect's designing and building a house without first consulting his clients about their likes and interests. This should not be interpreted to mean that the teacher must start anew each time, but that his resources and materials need to be adapted to the individual needs of the children he will be teaching.

A sound program of pupil appraisal and evaluation of the program is *much more comprehensive* than what is commonly termed a "testing program." Instruments and procedures that may be useful include observations, listening and recording, special ability scales, autobiographies and diaries, sociograms, intelligence, aptitude, achievement and teacher-made tests, as well as others.

The purpose of appraisal and evaluation is the better planning of programs and instruction, and the improvement of learning. However, when these procedures are utilized to classify or to attempt long-term homogeneous grouping, serious damage to the children involved may occur. Using tests for comparing one child to another or one group to another violates sound mental health principles since it usually serves to degrade and demean, and frequently causes a great many children to feel inferior. At its worst, it denies children equal educational opportunity because it predetermines the material they will have an opportunity to be exposed to and places a ceiling on the teacher's expectation of them. Evaluation and appraisal procedures must be planned so they encourage the teachers and, therefore, the pupils, to strive for greater skill and achievement.

The goals of the educational program determine the appraisal and evaluation instruments that are chosen. *Evaluation is obviously not an end in itself.* It must focus attention on:

a. The progress of the children toward the broad goals of the school.
b. Clarification of the success of the educational program, the methods, the learning techniques, and the activities that are being used to achieve these goals.
c. Identification of the problems that interfere with or prevent children from learning.
d. Providing the teacher and other school staff members with information for assisting students and guiding them toward objective goals.
e. Providing information which reveals evidence of growth for the purpose of indicating the success of the efforts of the faculty, pupils and parents.

2. CHARACTERISTICS OF A SOUND EVALUATION PROGRAM. There are a number of important characteristics that should be included in a sound appraisal and evaluation program. James Quillen and Lavonne A. Hanna[8] suggest the following:

a. "Evaluation includes all the means of collecting evidence on student behavior." This includes studies of the children's interests, histories, test results, anecdotal material, etc.
b. "Evaluation is concerned with the growth and the problems of each student rather than a comparison between him and other students, or between his group and other groups. If evaluation and appraisal is honestly for the purpose of improving the school program and helping children to achieve goals set for them, then except for statistical purposes, the major point of reference must be in relation to the progress the student is making and not to some hypothetical norm. It is unfortunate that

8 L. James Quillen and Lavonne A. Hanna, *Education for Social Competence* (New York: Scott, Foresman Co., 1948), pp. 343–46.

individuals who accept a physical educational program that does not produce all Olympic stars measure a school system's results in terms of how many Merit Scholars it produces.

c. "Evaluation is continuous; it is an integral part of all teaching and learning." Children and teachers evaluate themselves each day. Since learning itself is not terminal, neither is evaluation. Actually, evaluation is a concept, an ongoing process which continually determines the next steps for each teacher to provide or each child to choose.

d. "Evaluation is descriptive as well as quantitative." Human growth and development are so complex that test scores and comparisons are not adequate at this point to measure every nuance of behavior. The components of behavior are so interrelated that any one test score is influenced by many other factors and several test scores may be the result of having sampled the same behavior or influence on the same behavior. A multidimensional inventory is necessary to adequately describe growth and changes and problems related to pupil behavior, performance and skill. Even the best thought-out grade and numerical systems are not able to convey even a small part of the total behavior of a child.

e. "Evaluation is global in addition to being specific." Although the teacher may be looking for the cause of one problem in learning or evaluating one area of performance or skill, he must always obtain as global a picture of the child as possible. Too frequently, teachers ascribe a behavior characteristic to a specific cause without having considered the many dimensions that contribute to the uniqueness of this child's behavior.

f. "Evaluation is a cooperative process involving students, teachers, other school personnel, and parents." Students' performance in school is affected by all that troubles their lives. Things around them change, and in order to study this ongoing change, all of the elements in their environment should be considered. Since the learner learns best when he is personally involved and since he knows a great deal more about himself than anyone else, the evaluation must include him. He must recognize the goals, the part that evaluation plays in his achieving these goals, and he must have an important role in determining both the goals and how he reaches them. Self-appraisal is an increasingly important part of the entire appraisal process. The measure of the students' cooperation in the process may determine its success.

3. THE DEVELOPMENT OF A PUPIL APPRAISAL AND EVALUATION PROCESS. The development of a comprehensive process requires a carefully worked-out procedure. The following is suggestive of some of the steps:[9]

a. The goals of the school must be clearly stated as specific objectives and grouped so that those types of behavior that are related are grouped. The selection of evaluation instruments is governed by these objectives. The development and acceptance of a list of objectives by the staff of the school help to coordinate their efforts in relation to instructional programs and evaluation.

b. The objectives of the school must be stated in terms of behavior. A goal or objective is usually an end result to a sequence of learning experiences. The objectives must be stated in terms of recognizable behavior and broken down into short steps. If the objectives remain vague, there is no evaluative process that can determine whether or not they have been reached. The teacher

[9] Henry W. Magnuson and others, "Evaluating Pupil Progress," California State Department of Education, Vol. XXI, No. 6, April 1952, The Department, Sacramento, pp. 5–7.

must always ask for a specific statement of behavior for each objective if he hopes to plan experiences to achieve them. Objectives such as "good citizenship" and "the ability to use numbers" are too broad to be used meaningfully. Statements about behavior must be based upon a thorough knowledge of child growth and development. The background of the particular students must also be considered because of the sociological and psychological components of behavior.

c. The teacher must plan the experiences in which the students will have an opportunity to learn the behavior suggested as a goal. Certain experiences are real to children and offer a great opportunity to learn certain types of behavior. The school must list these experiences in a form such as "persistent life situations"[10] or "developmental tasks"[11] to assist students in developing certain proficiencies.

d. Instruments and techniques which assist in obtaining a comprehensive appraisal of the student must be employed. Having determined and listed the behavior that indicates that objectives and goals are being reached, the teacher must find instruments and techniques that have been developed to measure this behavior. The development of new instruments or informal appraisals may be necessary.

4. THE INTERPRETATION OF THE EVALUATION INSTRUMENTS AND TECHNIQUES. The ultimate purpose of the entire pupil appraisal and evaluation process is the improvement of the instructional program so that each student reaches his highest level of skill in every area. The process is useful only when it provides the school with the information necessary to

10 Florence B. Stratemeyer and others, *op. cit.*
11 Robert J. Havinghurst, *Developmental Tasks and Education,* 2nd ed. (New York, Longmans, Green & Co., 1952), p. 4.

improve its program. Even when a careful selection of instruments and techniques has been made, and they are proficiently used, their relative value is subject to the vagaries of interpretation. Interpretation is a key step to the use of the information. A number of dangerous errors may occur:

a. Interpretations are made from instruments or techniques which are not specifically spelled out in their purpose.
b. Interpretations are made from one instrument or technique, which is then generalized beyond any reasonable possibilities.
c. Data from one or more instruments and techniques used are not related to others, or the converse—data from unrelated instruments are woven together.
d. Interpretations are made without knowledge of child growth and development and causes of particular learning problems.

The gathering and interpretation of data is only an intellectual exercise and a façade for not knowing what to do unless it is put to use in a carefully planned instructional program. The ability to translate these findings for actual classroom use is a skill often lacking in classroom teachers and others having responsibility for evaluation and program planning.

Data to Be Collected

1. ANECDOTAL RECORDING OF CHILD OBSERVATION DATA. Careful observation of behavior is important in order to assess the success of each child in a program and for planning the particular activities which help to reach the educational goals the teacher has set for him. The underlying principle in observing children is that all behavior is purposeful and all action is caused. The teacher observes the children in or-

der to determine the status of their development and skill, their best methods of learning and to determine whether or not they have any problems which interfere with their success in school.

When a child performs a particular act, it is his effort to meet some subconscious or conscious need. In some cases, even when observing the child performing this action, one cannot easily determine what need is being fulfilled. When he is having difficulties, a child often behaves in such a manner that it appears he is acting in a way that is diametrically opposite of what he should do to accomplish a particular purpose. The teacher should try to get an idea of how the youngster observes the world, how he feels about things around him, how he attempts to overcome the problems that he faces and thinks are important. Based upon these observations, a thorough knowledge of child growth and development, of how children learn, and the techniques for helping each child, the teacher plans the types of experiences that each child needs, enabling him to succeed in his present environment as well as in his life in the future.

The teacher looks for clues in the child's behavior, little nuances that indicate what his interests might be, how he feels about himself and others, how he feels about the schoolwork, etc.

a. *Motivation:* What is he motivated to do? Is he highly motivated in some areas but not in others? What is his ambition? What things does he value most? How can he be influenced?

b. *Abilities and skills:* On what level is he functioning in various areas? Does he think abstractly or concretely? Is he able to take and respond to complicated directions?

c. *Emotional attitudes:* How does he express emotion? Does the emotion expressed appear to be related to what caused it? Does it disappear very quickly? Does he have

unusual behavior, such as nail-biting, or crying, which
may be emotionally based? How does he respond to
failure situations?

d. *Social relationships:* Does he get along with other children? What is his status with others? Does he play well
in the group? How does he indicate what his self-concept is?

e. *Physical characteristics:* Does he use his body well? Are
his large muscles and small muscles developed? Does
he have any perceptual learning problems or obvious
handicapping conditions?

f. *Past experience:* Are there clues in his behavior and his
discussions to indicate that he has had a wide variety of
experiences?

The objective of the observations must be clear. The
teacher should relate his observation to some goal, such as
how he can help improve the child's interest in books. His
reports concerning the child form an essential part of any
evaluation. The ability of the classroom teacher to observe
and record objectively and accurately is an important skill.

There are a number of guidelines that the teacher can
use to help him in the process of observation and recording.
In observing children, the teacher can choose some special
times or he can simply observe at random without any time
limitations. The number and range of observations will depend to a considerable extent on the objective to be reached,
the specific problem area, or a particular curriculum goal. If
observations are made comparing one child to others to determine the effect of certain experiences, they should be
made during similar activities so that each child has relatively the same experience.

In observing the child, the teacher is frequently attempting
to determine the cause for a certain pattern of behavior or the
reason for failure in relation to a certain school objective. It

is assumed that by observing the behavior of a pupil, we can help determine the nature and extent of a particular problem or the progress a child is making. In order for the teacher to be able to suggest some objective conclusion, he must obtain samples of behavior in a variety of situations. Unfortunately, too many teachers are prone to make broad generalizations or draw conclusions regarding the behavior of a pupil which are based upon the flimsiest, most fragmentary, or intangible evidence. The teacher must guard against considering only the behavior of the child when he is in charge of the situation. Children frequently act quite different when the teacher is not in the immediate vicinity. Sometimes the most threatening question for a teacher to ask himself is, Why have you come to this conclusion?

In order to avoid subjective and uninformed observations and judgments, observational skills constantly must be improved. Training in observation and recording techniques should be an important part of each teacher's education. This training should seek to sharpen the teacher's skill in judging the type and extent of the observation to be recorded and in being able to improve his accuracy when reporting his observations of pupil behavior. These records are usually more important and have broader implications than the observations that can be made during short visits by other staff members.

Observers have a tendency to make errors when reporting a situation. The following points are a summary of the more common errors that were found in stories told by witnesses who observed an automobile accident. This is indicative of the complexity of objectively evaluating children in complex situations:

a. Observers make symptomatic and related errors rather than random ones.

b. Observers tend to make biased judgments and then record observations that support their judgments.

c. Observers appear to be more sensitive to certain kinds of behavior than to others. They record what they feel is significant, overlooking or ignoring other observations.

d. Rather than remaining objective, observers tend to interpret what they see, and facts which do not fit their idea of the occurrence may be discarded.

e. The longer the time between observation and reporting, the greater the error. Important elements of the observation may be forgotten if they are not called to the attention of the observer at the time they occur.[12] (Note the immediate debriefing of astronauts.)

In order to reduce observer errors which will distort the objective picture of the child, the following techniques are suggested:

a. A time sample (in which the teacher observes a pupil for a given period of time at a particular hour for a number of days).

b. Using a diagram that follows a child's actions in a pictorial fashion helps give a more complete picture. For example:

9:10 Sat in his seat	9:15 Poked Sam as he walked by; no observable counterreaction	9:17 Settled down to read book
9:12 Took a book from library	9:16 Disturbed Jane in the seat next to him	9:18 Ran up to my desk with a picture he had found of a turtle in a book

---

12 Lee Cronbach, *Essentials of Psychological Testing* (New York, Harper Brothers, 1949), pp. 387–389.

c. Observations should be planned and made at various times of the day to get a total picture rather than only when the teacher finds he has a few moments.

d. It is important that the teacher plan his observations and that he adhere to that plan as closely as possible.

e. Short, closely spaced observations are apparently more significant to the total picture than an equal amount of observation time utilizing few observations and longer periods of time (during a number of days rather than a number of weeks).

f. In order to minimize forgetting, data must be recorded as soon after the observation as is possible.[13]

Thus we find that a written record of the child's behavior in a number of different situations under different sets of circumstances can give us insights we might not otherwise have. Teachers can begin to see a problem in perspective and seek to enlist the assistance of other school staff when necessary. Teachers are frequently surprised that as they study the anecdotal record over a period of time, a pattern occurs which can help them in finding ways to help the child. A sample of an observation record form appears in Figure II.

FIGURE II
OBSERVATION RECORD

NAME _____ DATE _____

SITUATION (During reading, art, etc.) _____

TIME STARTED _____ LENGTH OF TIME OBSERVED _____

OBJECTIVE DESCRIPTION OF BEHAVIOR _____

_____

_____

_____

[13] *Ibid.*, p. 390.

2. LISTENING TO CHILDREN AND KEEPING A RECORD OF WHAT THEY SAY. Listening is another technique for obtaining a comprehensive picture of a child and becoming acquainted with him. Frequently teachers are too busy planning, instructing, telling, marking, etc., to pay attention to what a child says. Talking to the child on an informal basis frequently helps the teacher gain insight into the child's behavior and his ideas and feeling about the things around him. The teacher may learn that a child sees his work in a confused manner and thus gain a clue about his behavior toward it. Talks with children probably help the teacher most when they appear to occur spontaneously and in an informal manner so that the child does not become self-conscious and the discussion strained and distorted. At first children often tell the teacher what they think he wants to hear. Special times that lend themselves to informal discussion and listening include intervals before and after school, when the child is helping around the room; club periods; lunch time; on the playground, and times when the child has completed his work. In some instances, the child actually seeks the teacher and discusses some extremely important confidential bit of information. The child who feels that the teacher is interested in him is more likely to have discussions which are informative insofar as understanding the child is concerned.

Children may talk about themselves, their families, things that happen around them, their feelings about things and people, their hopes, etc. All of these assist the teacher in obtaining a multidimensional view of the child. While a teacher can sometimes guide a child when they are discussing a particular subject, he must be careful not to appear to be prying or directing the child's behavior. The teacher's function is to be sympathetic and interested, encouraging the child to bring out his ideas. It is better to wait for further opportunities than try to do too much at one time. In order to help children who are reticent or withdrawn, the teacher must build up and communicate a feeling of *acceptance and trust* without which warmth and sympathy are of no value. After a number of successful experiences with the teacher, all but the most reluctant children will begin to engage the teacher in conversation. Gradually, these discussions will have great significance for the child.

The wise teacher plans chores (e.g., those before or after school) that bring the child in close contact with him. In each activity, the teacher gains another opportunity to get to know the child, while the child has an opportunity to know the teacher in an informal situation.

Finally, the teacher plans group and individual discussions around topics like What Do I Like to Do Most?, What Is the Most Exciting Thing That Happened to Me?, and he listens to each child. The manner in which the child brings out his ideas is also important for the teacher to observe. Some children thrive during these exploratory activities, while others indicate considerable resistance to participating.

3. RATING SCALES. A rating scale is a useful tool in the hands of a conscientious and objective observer. It can help to make observations more objective. Some ratings suggest dimensions of pupil behavior that the teacher might ordinarily overlook. As with any instrument of this nature, errors can occur both when the observer is at fault or when the scale itself does not adequately define the behavior to be reported upon.

A number of other limitations of the rating scale must be recognized by the teacher. Ratings on one part of the scale appear to influence those on other parts of the scale. Children with a problem in one area are sometimes rated as having problems in other areas, while children doing well in one area are also given the benefit of a doubt in another. Since we are usually attempting to get an overall picture of a child, stereotyped errors which suggest sweeping generalizations can occur. When teachers do the rating they sometimes respond to an item without objective evidence to back up their response, often because they feel the need to respond to all items.

Differing definitions of terms can frequently cause disagreement among ratings. An example may be that one teacher sees a cooperative child as one who agrees with him all the time, while to another it means being energetic and thoughtful, and showing evidence of leadership.

Some teachers are quite optimistic in their rating while others tend to rate everyone rather low. It should be obvious to the rater that a normal curve cannot be applied to a class since such a distribution normally requires a large number of children.

Of course, the most serious error that can occur comes from the teachers' own lives. Some teachers dislike some children, and like others. In many cases they feel this way for reasons that they may not be aware of. These subconscious feelings create a distorted picture of certain children as the teacher uses the rating scale or any other evaluative instrument that has a subjective component.

Although new rating scales are constantly being developed, many scales already available can be profitably used by an interested teacher. A school, or a school system, would find that a faculty study of various rating scales for teachers' use can be a worthwhile learning experience for the teachers, and the resultant combinations of scales can help improve evaluation and instruction. Rating scales have been developed to evaluate personality, work habits, social effectiveness, self-respect, interests and behavior as well as other areas.

An example of a rating scale which can be used by the teacher and may also serve as a teaching device with the students is the Self-Rating Character Chart, Figure III, which was developed to help students evaluate themselves. A scale from 1–5 was used to describe the frequency of trait occurrence:

1. Never
2. Almost Never
3. Sometimes
4. Frequently
5. Always

FIGURE III
SELF-RATING CHARACTER CHART[14]
(May be used by teachers for student rating)

I. RESPONSIBILITY: A responsible pupil does the following:
___ 1. Develops an interest and a will to learn
___ 2. Hands in schoolwork on time
___ 3. Comes to class on time
___ 4. Returns borrowed books promptly and in good condition
___ 5. Can be trusted while the teacher is out of the room
___ 6. Brings necessary equipment to class
___ 7. Asks no questions of his classmates during a test
___ 8. Is honest in preparing his own assignments
___ 9. Takes good care of school building, equipment, and grounds
___10. Does not waste school supplies
___11. Prepares and brings to class extra materials
___12. Accepts responsibility for developing projects helpful to the class
___13. Finds his own material for reports and other activities

[14] "Self-Rating Character Chart," Los Angeles Public Schools, 1949, in *Evaluating Pupil Progress* by Henry W. Magnuson and others. California State Department of Education, Sacramento, Vol. XXI, No. 6, April 1952.

II. COOPERATION: A cooperative student does the following:
  __ 1. Listens when someone is talking
  __ 2. Does not talk to other pupils unnecessarily
  __ 3. Cooperates with class officers and committee chairmen
  __ 4. Enriches the work of the class by bringing books, pictures, and other aids
  __ 5. Respects opinions of others
  __ 6. Controls his voice and actions
  __ 7. Abides by group decisions
  __ 8. Does nothing which will bring criticism on his class or school

III. WORK HABITS: A student possessing good work habits does the following:
  __ 1. Starts to work promptly and does not waste time
  __ 2. Hands in written assignments promptly
  __ 3. Does his work accurately
  __ 4. Gets to work without urging by the teacher
  __ 5. Completes assignments before coming to class
  __ 6. Is careful to follow directions
  __ 7. Uses intelligently the index, table of contents, and dictionaries
  __ 8. Prepares reports in his own words
  __ 9. Enunciates words distinctly
  __10. Pronounces words accurately
  __11. Prepares written work neatly

The checklist is another type of rating scale, although more limited, and it is much easier to use. The teacher merely checks the qualities of a child from a list. Although it is a simple device, it can help the teacher to get some idea, in a rather quick and easy fashion, of a child's pattern of work and personality and an indication of his growth.

There are many different types of checklists. Some may be developed in cooperation with students so they understand the meaning of each term. Children can be asked to describe people who have these traits. They may be devised to meet specific situations or attempt to cover overall behavior. Figure IV is an example of such a checklist. It is "Check List to Report Evidence of Pupil Responsibility, Co-operation, Self-Respect, and Social Concern."[15]

FIGURE IV

CHECK LIST TO REPORT EVIDENCE OF PUPIL RESPONSIBILITY, CO-OPERATION, SELF-RESPECT, AND SOCIAL CONCERN

I. RESPONSIBILITY
   A. Takes care of self
   ___1. Keeps promises   ___4. Thinks of self
   ___2. Is trustworthy   ___5. Remembers for self
   ___3. Owns up   ___6. Is dependable

   B. Does own part and shares
   ___1. Keeps on until   ___3. Shows good manners
        finished   ___4. Is a good leader
   ___2. Always does best   ___5. Is a good follower

II. CO-OPERATION
   A. Follows directions
   ___1. Does what the teacher   ___3. Plays games willingly
        suggests   ___4. Finishes on time
   ___2. Does all of the ques-
        tions at the end of
        lessons

   B. Is quiet
   ___1. Gives others a chance   ___4. Doesn't crowd
   ___2. Takes turns   ___5. Keeps voice low
   ___3. Doesn't bother   ___6. Listens
        neighbors

15 *Santa Barbara County Program of Evaluation: Developing Concepts, Attitudes, and Skills,* Vol. 8. Prepared under the direction of the Office of the County Superintendent of Schools, Santa Barbara County. (Santa Barbara, California, Schauer Printing Studio, Inc., 1945) , p. 143.

C. Takes care of supplies

__1. Doesn't make pictures when supposed to be studying

__2. Takes good care of books

III. SELF-RESPECT

__A. Owns up

__B. Is honest

__C. Plays fair

__D. Is prompt

__E. Is willing

__F. Obeys

__G. Does his best

__H. Shows self-control

__ I. Thinks of others

__ J. Is a good sport

__K. Gives ideas

__L. Shares

__M. Does things for others

IV. SOCIAL CONCERN

__A. Brings things to decorate the room

__B. Brings things to help a committee

__C. Does good turns for others

__D. Lets others do good turns for him

__E. Is thoughtful

4. THE SOCIOGRAM. An important part of each student's life concerns his relationship to his peers and thus this becomes an important school goal. The sociogram is a technique which can be used to diagram and study these social relationships. Children can be given an opportunity of making choices involving their classmates as well as others. They may be asked to list their three best friends, the two or three people they would most like to work with, go on a picnic with, have on their team or the most popular children in the class. Children have been found to choose different children for different activities.

Although their choices may vary from day to day, there are a number of reasons why the type of information to be gained from a sociogram can be very important. There are some children who are easily accepted by others, while others find it more difficult to make and to hold onto friends. Since it is important for every child to have an opportunity to find his place in his peer group, finding out the relationships that exist is essential. Those who have had experience with children are aware of the unhappiness that children feel when they are rejected or ignored by other children. This frustration may cause a child to behave quite erratically in the classroom. He may act out aggressive behavior and create disturbances or he may withdraw, creating his own world of friends. As a result of studying the friendship and grouping patterns of the class, the teacher can sometimes arrange for play activities which will encourage the group to include each child. If the child has some ability, talent or interest, the teacher may also find techniques for giving the student an opportunity to show these to the class and perhaps to gain their approval and acceptance.

In the lower grades, the teacher can chart the socio-pattern by privately asking each child to indicate his choice, while in the higher grades children can fill in the information on prepared sheets.

Since different situations may call for different grouping, the teacher would be wise to indicate a specific situation when asking students to indicate their choices. The choice of the situation is important. It must be meaningful to the student and present him with an opportunity to make a free selection. It is understood that the teacher must make it clear that the information is strictly confidential, will not be evaluated in any way detrimental to the student, and will result in improved friendliness in the classroom.

Discussion should be discouraged since it tends to limit the choices. Periodic reassessment will indicate changes and the effectiveness of the teacher's efforts to help children who have been isolated.

The teacher can diagram the children and their choices for

a graphic view of the class relationships. There are a number of items the teacher should be looking for:

a. What are the bases for the choices? Are they the result of classroom arrangement, proximity of living, nationality, color, religion, academic ability, etc.?
b. Who are the children most and least often chosen?
c. Note the one-way relationships which show a child reaching out, and the two-way group that closes out one or more children.
d. What are the common characteristics of the children chosen most often? Ability, color, achievement, sports ability, church group, attendance, etc.?
e. What are the common characteristics of children chosen least often? Newness to the school, poor behavior, non-participation in outside activities, etc.?
f. Does the class grouping reflect the separation of groups within the community?[16]

The teacher's choice of the "star" might not be the student chosen by the class. The basis for the choice of leader varies from age to age and from group to group. While one age group might select the student who is outstanding in school-work, another might choose the athletic leader; and a group of children from homes in poorer neighborhoods might choose the child who is strongest or has the most cunning.

As the teacher becomes skilled in his use of the results of the sociogram for planning activities, he will have greater success in eliminating the problem of the child who is isolated or rejected. He will improve the opportunities for developing satisfactory personal relationships, making them available to more children, and he will be more successful in achieving one of the major goals in education.

16 *Sociometry in Group Relations,* American Council on Education, Washington, D.C., 1948, pp. 28–29.

5. AUTOBIOGRAPHIES AND DIARIES. In attempting to get as complete a picture of each child as he can, the teacher may want to use autobiographical and diary material. Utilizing this technique enables him to observe the child in an area where he has an opportunity to express his own ideas freely. Frequently, the child's significant feelings are exposed through this avenue.

The child's autobiographical sketch of himself often reveals his life as he interprets it. It supplements other information and evidence that the teacher has gathered. It may indicate attitudes toward himself, his family, the school, playmates, his problem, disabilities, etc. Since the biographical sketch is historical in nature, the student may have forgotten the exact details of what has happened and thus interpret the events in terms of his present needs. The student is encouraged to write about his home life, childhood experiences, school activities, personal interests, friends and future plans.

In contrast to the autobiography, the diary is a daily account of activities. This is the student's personal interpretation of his experiences and observations. Although the activities recorded are usually related to school, the diary may also include other people and events about which he feels concerned. The diary may sometimes help the pupil to obtain a better self-appraisal and more insight into his behavior problems. If the student is really willing to write freely, the diary can help illuminate hidden causes for behavior, attitudes about himself and others, as well as what he thinks are his real problems.

6. TESTING THE PUPIL'S PRESENT ACADEMIC AND OTHER SKILL LEVELS: GROUP TESTS. In administering any type of formal test, the teacher or the examiner must make certain that the conditions under which the test is given are those called for by the instrument. Any deviation raises serious questions regarding the interpretation of the test.

Care must be taken to choose appropriate tests. A test based almost entirely on material that evaluates the verbal skills of children discriminates against those who have a language problem, who use a foreign language in the home, or who live in homes that do not use verbal language. The selection of the test must be directly related to what is being measured. If the teacher knows that the child has a language problem, it is ridiculous to choose a test which only proves this. It would be more appropriate to choose a test which helps to suggest the child's strength and one which helps to diagnose the specific language problems of the child. Theoretically, tests are not constructed to fail children but rather to determine their strengths and analyze their difficulties. On the contrary, if the teacher knows a child will do very badly on a test, it probably should never be administered.

a. *Achievement tests:* Achievement tests have usually been standardized with large populations. Usually, every attempt is made by the publisher to have the sample be truly representative of the general school population.

Since these tests are utilized for the purpose of evaluating the pupil's level of achievement and the progress he has made, it is important to choose an instrument whose goals are in line with those of the school. Unfortunately, as is the case with other evaluation instruments, teachers frequently misunderstand their use and function. They sometimes misinterpret the concept of the norm, which is really only the average measure of an unselected group of children. Some school systems take credit for having a great percentage of their students achieve above the norm, but the fact is that this above-normal achievement is probably largely related to the type of community the child lives in and the education and income levels of the family rather than the education the child is receiving. Likewise, if students achieve scores which are below the norm, it does not usually mean that the school is at fault. Differences in overall scores may be the result of the children's environment, the length of the school year, the emphasis the school has in certain areas, the teachers' ability, etc.

Sometimes it appears that the entire education program in a school system is geared toward training its students to make high scores on a particular set of achievement tests. This is certainly a case of the tail wagging the dog. The test should not determine the program of the school. On the contrary, tests should be carefully chosen so that they measure the achievement of the goals that are set by the school. Certainly, all of the staff in a system should have a hand in planning which tests are to be used.

Achievement tests should be given early in the school year, so that the teacher has an opportunity to utilize the information provided for instruction, not at the end so they appear to threaten the teacher, who may then teach for them. Group achievement tests are useful for obtaining an overall picture of the children tested so that plans can be made for them. The group test has not been designed for use as an individual diagnostic instrument and when it is so used, serious errors in interpretation can occur. When a student receives a low score on a particular subject, the competent teacher looks into the reasons more closely and asks for a diagnostic assessment before proceeding to develop materials to aid him. The achievement test can be helpful only when it is used within specific limitations.

b. *Special aptitude tests:* Tests have been developed to measure the special aptitudes of children. These tests assist the teacher in finding children who may have talent in music and art, and aptitudes in mechanical or scientific areas. While it is difficult to administer aptitude tests to all children, they can be used in individual cases when the teacher thinks they are warranted.

c. *Readiness tests:* Readiness tests may be considered a specialized form of aptitude test. The readiness test attempts to define the child's state of readiness for a particular field. Reading is the field in which the most extensive work has been done, although other areas, including physical education and arithmetic readiness, are being explored. Such tests are designed to evaluate the areas which are related to the subject under consideration. Strengths and weaknesses are examined so that plans to take advantage of the strengths and to ameliorate, remediate or circumvent the weaknesses are made. In evaluating a child's readiness, it is important that consideration be given to all areas of his function. Investigation of problems in physical as well as emotional areas should be carried out.

The readiness tests may be helpful in bringing out problem areas but they do not describe the action to be taken. Scores on these specialized tests are not as important as the information they provide regarding particular problems.

d. *Teacher-made skill and achievement tests:* The accomplishment of many of the school goals cannot be measured on formal tests. The teacher evaluates the progress the child is making through the utilization of the procedures previously mentioned. He observes, checks, discusses, listens, etc. In addition, he also evaluates the pupil's performance in his class in relation to improvement in the use of skills and gains in the areas of information the school feels he may need.

The teacher-made skill and information tests must be constructed to measure specific goals, usually short-term goals. These tests frequently form a large part of the evaluation of each child. The teacher who feels responsible for helping each child progress as rapidly and as far as possible gears his program to the needs of each child. The program is based in large measure on the results of the child's performance on the evaluation instrument.

A number of different skills and methods of learning can be gained during these informal tests, depending on the technique the teacher asks the child to use to respond to the items. Unfortunately, the techniques the child must use frequently bear little relationship to the goals of education.

Most teacher-made tests (and others) ask the child to recall a specific piece of information, recognize which of two, three or four answers is correct, or match the question and the answer. The fact that the child can perform these tasks on the test may have little to do with his understanding of or his ability to use the information or skill.

The open-end essay question, the essay question that asks the students to compare, the open-end problem question, the requirements of a problem-solving approach, the creative-use question are much more related to the skills the child needs and measure the child's understanding to a greater degree.

Tests of recognition—those that use multiple-choice, matching and true-false questions—are the type most popular with teachers because of their ease of construction and scoring. However, these contribute to the worst form of learning. Instead of measuring understanding, they stress memorization and guessing, and may lead the young child to erroneous conclusions and sometimes to cheating. A true-false question may well leave the child believing the false statement because it is written and given to him by the teacher.

Written tests are not the only form of teacher-made tests. Problem-solving situations can be presented to children in an attempt to evaluate their skills in critical thinking, judgment, logical reasoning, using skills and information to solve a problem, making and testing a hypothesis, interpreting new material, drawing conclusions, and applying generalizations to new situations.

A written record of the child's performance in these areas can be extremely important in helping the teacher evaluate the child's progress and determine the nature and extent of problems that may interfere with reaching the goals.

Behavior That Signals the Need for a Special Evaluation

Part of a comprehensive evaluation design includes a procedure which provides for a staff of pupil personnel specialists, members of other community agencies who preside over a series of specific diagnostic instruments and tests which are used to attempt to find the causes of special problems, and who recommend proper ameliorative procedures, special treatments, equipment or programs.

The following are some of the types of behavior that should lead the teacher to request a complete evaluation to determine the specific cause for the learning problem. Since it is possible that the removal of a physical problem may assist in eliminating the problem in learning, the first evaluation to recommend is usually medical. Some situations such as epileptic seizures, loss of parts of the body, blindness, etc., are not listed because they are obvious. Some behavior which should act as a signal to the teacher is: (See Chapter 5 for discussion of causes.)

1. HEARING. Responds very poorly to spoken language or sound, holds head at peculiar angle to hear, has ear discharges, pain in the ear, etc.

2. SPEECH. Speech is quite unclear, pitched too high or low, too loud or soft, of monotonous quality, stutters, etc.

3. VISION. Strabismus (cross-eyed condition) , holding head at peculiar angle to see, rubbing eyes, squinting, awkward eye-hand coordination, complaints of inability to see, etc.

4. MOTOR. Unusual gait, peculiar sitting or standing positions, ungainly movement, etc.

5. BEHAVIOR. Easily overstimulated, hyperactive, unable to modify behavior, distractable, uneven rhythm to behavior, poor memory, creates serious disturbances, severely withdrawn, etc.

6. PERCEPTION. Seriously distorted handwriting, uneven response to spoken and/or written directions, unable to copy written material, etc.

It is important to note that some of these characteristics appear in children who have no physical damage and may be transitional or idiosyncratic in nature, and that some of them must be rather serious before a teacher should refer the child.

Most school systems have developed a simple referral form that is used by the teacher (see Figure V) . When a child has a persistent problem which interferes with his learning, the teacher should take careful, objective, observational notes so that accurate information can be transmitted to the referral source.

A comprehensive special educational evaluation includes developmental history, present and prior complaints, previous medical, educational, and therapeutic experiences, self-help and behavior, as well as specific investigation of perceptual functions, psycho-motor functions, language comprehension and usage, ability to communicate verbally and non-verbally, behavior, attitudes towards self and others, and feelings towards parents, family, school, spontaneity, and approach to a given task. When the child is of school age, specific academic areas are investigated according to the requirements usually expected of that particular chronological age. Often problems interweave. Primary dysfunctions may be accompanied by secondary problems in behavior which may be so severe at the time the child is first seen that these, even though not the original cause of difficulty, need attention first before any more specific educational plans can be made.[17]

Although some problems can be handled rather easily, most of them require a comprehensive evaluation, including consultation with a number of learning specialists.

FIGURE V
SPECIAL EVALUATION
TEACHER'S REFERRAL FORM

Child's Name _____ Date of Birth _____ Age __

Grade _____ Sex _____ School _____

Teacher _____ Date of Referral _____

Referral is made for the following reasons:

1. _____

2. _____

3. _____

Describe the child's behavior as related to the problem fully and in objective terms.

Teacher needs assistance in planning to deal with the following problems:

[17] Ruth Mallison, "Individual Educational Therapy for the Special Child," in *The Special Child in Century 21*, Jerome Hellmuth, ed. Seattle, The Special Child Publications, 1964.

A Comprehensive Psychological Evaluation

All too often, a child who is having a problem which interferes with his learning is given a group test of mental ability. This practice is presumed to describe the total picture of the child. Educators frequently use a poor result as an excuse for their failure to teach, unfortunately too often with the silent acquiescence of the psychologist or psychometrist.

A psychological report, if it is to have any value for the teacher, must go beyond the mere reporting of test scores or the restatement of the problems as the teacher presented them or as the tester observed them. The report must contain specific information in a form that makes it both comprehensible and useful for the purpose of placement and program planning. Harold Delp[18] suggests a number of specific problems to consider in the preparation of a useful report:

1. A complete picture of the child and how he is functioning must emerge from the psychological evaluation. All of the results must be brought together with general and specific patterns brought out.

2. The evaluator must not extend the information of the results beyond those which good procedure and his own experience suggest.

3. If adaptations in the use of the test have been made, they must be carefully explained. Feelings of uncertainty relating to certain findings should be noted and detailed in the report.

4. A score in terms of I.Q. or M.A. is rather meaningless without additional information. The examiner must take pains to de-emphasize the "numerical rating." In certain

---

[18] Harold A. Delp, "School Diagnosis of the Mentally Retarded: Interpretation and Report to Using Personnel," *The Training School Bulletin*, 52:9, January 1956, pp. 231–236.

cases, as with children who have had an injury to the brain, they are relatively meaningless.

5. The educator must use appropriate instruments. It is absurd to use the wrong one and explain why the results may not apply.

6. Classification of the student according to some system does not really give the teacher specific information. The examiner should explain the needs of the child in as many dimensions as possible.

(Author's note: Although the examiner may make some suggestions regarding placement, the decision is based upon educational considerations and is finally made by the school.)

All the above requires considerable familiarity with the child, the teacher and the school system. Observation of the child in the classroom situation would appear to be essential if recommendations regarding his function in school are to be made. The teacher must insist that the psychological evaluation is based upon and contains information that helps him work with the child. Nothing less is worthwhile.

The Comprehensive Medical Evaluation

The purpose of the comprehensive medical evaluation is to determine if there is a possible medical cause for the problem the child has; to suggest ameliorative procedures such as braces, learning aides, etc., or treatment such as drugs, vitamins, etc.; to record the medical history of the child; and to make specific recommendations concerning physical limitation of the child's program (e.g., rest periods, limited physical activity, etc.) if needed.

In many school systems, there is a requirement that all children have a periodic physical examination, supplemented by dental, hearing and vision evaluations. All too frequently, these represent a most superficial examination since the physician must see a great many children each day. Although some problems are discovered, this perfunctory evaluation necessarily overlooks others that could be found in a more exhaustive examination. When a child exhibits a problem in school, every attempt must be made to determine if a physical cause exists.

The physical examination usually is preceded by a reading of the complete medical history, obtained from a hospital, the family physician or the mother. When the school physician discovers or becomes aware of the possibility of more complicated problems, he will ask for such additional examinations as necessary. "Among the specialists that may be required on occasion are the ophthalmologist, otologist, and audiologist, otolaryngologist, pathologist, orthopedist or neurologist."[19]

These specialists make a thorough diagnosis in their special areas of competence, and if they find any specific problems, they may recommend certain specific medical steps and/or suggest the need for modification of the school program.

With serious problems, such as those in vision, hearing and speech, education specialists with skills in working with children in these areas may need to be brought into the program. For children with problems such as orthopedic impairment, out-of-school specialists (such as a physiotherapist) may be suggested.

The medical report should also be written in such language and contain such explanation that it can be interpreted by the teacher and the school administrator.

Evaluation of the Family Situation

In some instances, there may be no need to obtain a comprehensive family picture to ascertain the cause of the

[19] Orville G. Johnson, "Guidance for Exceptional Children" in William M. Cruickshank, and Orville G. Johnson, *Exceptional Children and Youth* (Englewood Cliffs, New Jersey, Prentice-Hall, 1958), p. 618.

problem because it is not related to the home. However, it is wise to obtain as much information as possible on a child's complete background and environment.

A staff member such as a social worker trained in understanding the family can provide the information needed. The report should contain a history of the individual in relation to his family and his neighborhood, the conditions at home, his feelings about his family, his adjustment to the elements in his environment, his level of maturation, as well as other pertinent information. All of these facts may be indicative of the child's growth in social and emotional areas and his ability to deal constructively with his home surroundings.

School Evaluation

The school evaluation is frequently the most ignored part of the study of a child. Frequently, we find a few marks and test scores on a cumulative record card and little else. While these bits of information can contribute to the evaluation of the child, they certainly do not form the complete educational picture.

The observations of the current teacher, the previous teacher, the school principal, and others of the school who have the contact with the children can offer the best information, and they can be of tremendous value in determining the nature and cause of a child's problem. It is important that the school build up a comprehensive record for each child if it attempts to help them on an individual basis. Minimally, the school should build such an evaluation for a child when it recognizes that he has a problem.

A Note About Intelligence Scores

Intelligence is the most frequent measure used to describe a child, any child, and it almost always appears in an evaluation of a child with a problem which interferes with his learning. While many psychologists and educators still argue that it is useful in some areas, its role has been greatly overplayed and it has been frequently misused. As additional information concerning the dimensions of the capabilities of children is accumulated, serious questions concerning the influence of the intelligence score are emerging.

The information which would fit what we currently know about intelligence tests can be stated as follows:

1. It is no longer tenable to hold that any intelligence score will remain stable throughout an individual's life. There is evidence that it can fluctuate widely, especially during the early years of life. It may go down as well as up. Until recently, if a child scored higher on a second test than he did on the first, we usually assumed that the original score was erroneous, for one reason or another, and that the more recent test was the correct one. If the new test was lower, we would usually accept the earlier one, but we might use the second for classification purposes. "The simplest way out of this situation is to admit that measurement of lifelong potential is not within the grasp of psychologists and is a mirage."[20] A number of studies have demonstrated that intervention at certain points can produce significant changes in the measured intelligence score.

2. The intelligence test takes only a sampling of a number of items which are assumed to be representative of an individual's total function. J. P. Guilford[21] has suggested many more dimensions to intelligence than are sampled in any test. The skills sampled on an intelligence test are usually performance, verbal aptitude or performance. The test presumes to measure the maximum ability of each child and thus pre-

[20] James J. Gallagher, and James W. Moss, "New Concepts of Intelligence and Their Effects on Exceptional Children," *Exceptional Children*, Sept. 1963, pp. 1–4.

[21] J. P. Guilford, "The Structure of Intellect," *Psychological Bulletin*, Vol. 53 (1956), pp. 267–293.

dicts future performances. The variability of results indicates the error in this line of thinking. Instead, we need to analyze the specific tasks the test is sampling and interpret these diagnostically for the teacher's use in the classroom.

3. The actual items of the test change from one age level to another and different cognitive abilities are sampled at different ages. A change in score may be due to the fact that different abilities are being measured rather than to a raising or lowering of intelligence. Tests measure a wide variety of skills and abilities. Frequently, the same test, the Stanford-Binet, for instance, introduces a new set of questions that sample an area that has not been tested at an earlier age. The fact that a child has achieved a certain level in an earlier skill is no guarantee that this child will achieve the same level in a new skill.

4. The intelligence test is more a measure of the information and experience that the individual has than of any other factor such as potential or innate ability.

Using the tests with children who have learning problems further complicates their usefulness. Children who lack the experience demanded by the test fail on these items, not because they do not have the capability, but because they do not have the experience to draw upon.

Some tests can measure achievement if a proper situation is constructed. They can be diagnostic if care is taken to administer them properly. They can be useful in measuring strengths and weaknesses if they are interpreted and utilized by the classroom teacher in her planning. They do describe what the child really is doing, not always what the child cannot do. We should not feel safe in using these I.Q. scores as a basis for predicting a child's achievement or for suggesting his specific inherited ability.

Finding a low score on an intelligence test is like having a physician find that a child has a high temperature. It tells him that there is something wrong with the system but it does not tell him what. He must use other tools and experience to determine the exact nature of the problem before he can suggest remedial measures or special treatment. He certainly does not assume that the temperature will not change.

Capacity and Ability

We are all concerned with helping each child to obtain the best education possible in the broadest sense of the term. However, in order to determine how a student is succeeding we constantly refer to his capacity or ability as if this were a carefully documented, specific state. It is obvious that we cannot ascertain the potential of an individual and it is a matter of record that we have always underestimated it.

Probably these concepts have gained acceptance because of our tremendous need to measure things and determine how successful we are. In the field of sports or science we hardly ever accept the terms *capacity* or *ability* as finite measures. When these terms are used, they are frequently proved to be incorrect. It was not too long ago that the statement "The four-minute mile is beyond the capacity of human beings" was accepted by the best athletes in the world, but an athlete who did not accept the limitation of human capacity came along and ran the mile in less than four minutes.

When a child who achieves an I.Q. score of 110 does work comparable to that of a student who scores 140, some people will discuss the problem of the "overachiever" as if he were performing above his potential or capacity; a ridiculous concept at best. While groups of intelligence scores are highly correlated to overall eventual achievement, they are not perfectly correlated for each individual, and there is evidence that we can change the eventual achievement and I.Q. scores through specialized teaching techniques.

Although it may be difficult to defend in its extreme,

teachers should operate on the premise that *any one can learn to do anything if the proper techniques are used to help him.* The teacher who decides that a child cannot learn frequently dooms him to an inferior status as a student and perhaps for life.

The Evaluation and Planning Team

The "team approach" has become a cliché. All too frequently, the team is composed of an administrator, a principal, and the psychologist or examiner, or a speech and hearing teacher. Depending on the problem, it may include a social worker, physician, etc. The psychologist or the speech and hearing teacher reports on the test and recommends placement in a program, and that is that.

To really be of value, the group of individuals meeting to discuss a child should bring particular information and skills related to the case. The interaction that takes place between the members can be the most valuable part of the conference. A "team" is more than a group of individuals—it represents a special working relationship among peers. The teacher (regular or special class, itinerant or home instruction) who will be responsible for the child should (1) obtain a clear understanding of the cause, if one is found, (2) its relation to the behavior of the child, (3) all the factors that impinge on the problem, (4) the steps that can or will be taken to solve the problem if it is medical, or if the solution is to be found out of school and most important, (5) specific insight in the behavior characteristics of the child, and (6) specific suggestions for helping the child in the school situation.

The decision concerning the program for the child should be the result of contributions of the members of the team. To be able to function in a coherent fashion, each member must have a clear idea of his role and its relationship to the entire procedure. Too often, there is a struggle to determine who is supposed to do what instead of a concentrated focusing on the child. This is unfortunate among professionals whose training has theoretically prepared them to work with others. In the author's opinion, it is important that there be agreement by the group that it is essential to work together toward the common goal rather than to struggle for a clear decision of what one can do as opposed to another. There is no best division of responsibilities. Each team is different from every other team and the best skills of each must be used if sound programs can be evolved for the children we are concerned with. The team is a structure in which each member is enabled and encouraged to make his unique contribution. The National Training Laboratory has experimented with techniques for helping a group of individuals become a team.[22]

Conclusion

The evaluation of children frequently becomes a method for determining who has made the "top" or the "best" performance. The teacher causes many children to be dissatisfied with what may be an excellent piece of work when he asks the class to choose the best story or the best drawing. Children who have been stimulated and have worked hard to produce sometimes do not get the recognition they deserve. Evaluation which is continuous helps the teacher to prevent work related to past performance, and where there is evidence of improvement in the qualities of persistence, concentration and work habits the child must be praised. The child must be provided with experiences that increase his self-confidence and self-respect and thus help him with the motivation and initiative to continue to improve.

It is essential to keep in mind, as we strive to help children

[22] L. P. Bradford, J. R. Gibb and K. D. Benne, eds., *T-Group Theory, and Laboratory Methods: Innovation in Re-education* (New York, John Wiley & Sons, 1964) .

achieve the goals we set, that children come to us to help them learn, not to see who is the best or to compete for grades. Evaluation and assessment instruments and techniques are worthwhile only when they assist us in helping children's growth and development. When they are used as weapons to force children to work harder, they are not only worthless but actually harmful.

CHAPTER 4

Problems Encountered in Achieving
the Goals of Education

There is a general sequence that each individual goes through as he lives and grows. While there are many specific differences, still each person has a number of similar experiences. Most of us learn to crawl, run, play ball, read a book, get a job, enjoy recreational activities and raise children. These are all the tasks of learning to live. While animals rely on natural maturation for learning to build a nest or to fear certain larger animals, human behavior is much more a product of learning.

At this point in our knowledge, *we do not know whether we really have any limitations on our capacity to learn, since there is no way of really measuring potential.* We do know that we have almost always underestimated our ability. Nature appears to have provided us with a wide range of potential abilities. The level to which these are developed is limited only by our maturation and our ability to find the right way to learn.

Rather than growing and learning in an even, smooth pattern, we achieve these in spurts, depending on a great many factors. As the child develops his various human talents, he encounters and learns to deal with or avoid problems produced by his environment. Since learning occurs throughout our entire lives, situations and experiences that influence us may occur at any time.

As the individual grows, he finds himself possessed of new physical and psychological resources. The infant's legs grow larger and stronger, enabling him to walk. The child's nervous system grows more complex, enabling him to reason more subtly and to understand the complexities of subjects such as arithmetic. The individual also finds himself facing new demands and expectations from the society around him.[23]

Some of the developmental stages are a result of the physical maturation of the individual. The time for learning to walk, talk or have sex relations occurs when the human being has developed to the necessary level.

Other requirements of behavior are determined by our social needs in a particular cultural setting. Children must learn to get along with others, read, write and play certain games because our society is organized so that individuals must develop along these lines to be successful. As they grow older, children have a greater role to play in determining their further development. A child may decide whether he wants to spend his time learning to read better, becoming more proficient in baseball, or fishing.

As we observe the stages of learning, we become aware of their complexity and the large number of factors which influence successful development.

Our awareness that a child has a problem which prevents his reaching the goal which has been set is the first step in overcoming the problem. In order to deal with the problem, the teacher must next state the problem in precise terms. (*Inadequate:* Jimmy makes mistakes in reading; *Better:* Jimmy skips words in oral reading; *Inadequate:* Jane gets out

[23] Robert J. Havighurst, *Development Tasks and Education,* 2nd ed. (New York, Longmans, Green and Co., 1952), p. 4.

of her seat; *Better:* Jane moves out of her seat every five minutes, whether or not she has work to do.)

His next step is to identify the goal in relation to the problem. In Jimmy's case, this might be more accurate oral reading and in Jane's case, it might be better concentration or better self-control. It is important that the goal be determined, since the inappropriateness of the goal for this child may be the cause of the problem. In addition, when the goal is specific, the teacher may be able to develop alternate techniques for achieving it.

This chapter utilizes Florence Stratemeyer's concept of "building understandings, values and skills through experiences arising out of the daily situations children and youth face and using persistent life situations—the recurring situations which are the constants in a changing world—as the guides to the direction in which experiences should be developed."[24]

The activities that are planned for children in school should be derived from a statement of the goals sought. One method for stating these goals is in terms of the behavior that is expected of each individual in relation to situations he will meet throughout his entire life. Although these goals do not coincide with traditional curriculum patterns, they can be identified as part of them. The outline can be used to identify major areas of concern. Specific experiences must be developed if they are to be useful.

A wide variety of problems which prevent the child from achieving the goals sought are possible. The following outline gives examples of a number of these problems. Neither the list of goals nor the list of problems is meant to be exhaustive. They are intended merely to suggest some that the teacher might want to know about in order to help children

[24] Florence B. Stratemeyer and others, *Developing a Curriculum for Modern Living,* 2nd ed. (New York: Bureau of Publications, Teachers College, Columbia University, 1957), p. 161. Reprinted by permission.

when they encounter problems in attempting to achieve these goals.

I. Situations Calling for Growth in Individual

A. Health

1. Satisfying physiological needs
   a. Meeting food needs (e.g., eats inappropriate food; overeats)
   b. Securing needed rest and activity (e.g., tires easily; is lethargic; does not use facilities for relaxation and activity)
   c. Meeting sex needs (e.g., performs actions out of keeping with sex role)
   d. Getting rid of body wastes (e.g., has lapses in control of elimination of body wastes)
   e. Using body properly (e.g., has poor knowledge of how body parts are related; has poor image of body as physical entity; cannot see relationship of objects to self; makes poor use of body)

2. Satisfying emotional and social needs
   a. Achieving self-acceptance and securing relations with others (e.g., has no friends—unable to establish affectionate relationships, is not chosen by others; unable to achieve status in groups; unwilling to try new experiences or work; cannot accept kidding when directed at himself; is too concerned about being good; refuses to acknowledge weaknesses, inability or failure)
   b. Making constructive use of emotions (e.g., must always win—be first; does not accept variations in satisfaction; inappropriate emotional reactions to instruction or assigned tasks—screams, tears up papers, etc.; is withdrawn and shy; is aggressive; has extreme mannerisms—nail-biting, hair-twisting, finger sucking, etc.; is usually unhappy, becomes ill without apparent reason)

c. Achieving self-direction and independence (e.g., cannot decide when he has a choice; does not go about solving a problem logically; unable to resolve conflict situations; constantly asking teacher for support for his behavior and work; cries when separated from parent or teacher; does not complete assigned work; inconsistent performance—passes one, fails next, passes, fails, etc.)

3. Avoids and cares for illness
   a. Avoiding illness (e.g., does not practice desirable cleanliness, health routines; exposes himself to situations which can lead to illness)
   b. Avoiding accidents (e.g., careless—does not seem to consider his own safety)
   c. Caring for physical defects (e.g., does not accept limitation placed upon him by physical defects; has poor balance; uses physical disability as a crutch to evade responsibility; is obese)

B. Problems in Developing Intellectual Power

1. Making ideas clear
   a. Using spoken language to communicate (e.g., has inappropriate speech or language patterns for age and sex; spells too fast or too slow; uses inappropriate language—slang, hip language; uses oral language infrequently; does not make oral presentations when appropriate—cannot make reports of activities, etc.; considerable hesitation when asked a question; responds with a question; speaks without expression)
   b. Using written language to communicate (e.g., makes letter and number reversals in writing; does not express ideas in written form; is not careful in spelling during writing; hand writing is relatively illegible—writes too large, poor coordination, wanders, does not stay on lines; cannot write own name and address; unable to express a complete sentence

or thought in writing; cannot make transition from manuscript to cursive written language; does not use punctuation or uses it incorrectly; has trouble following written directions)

c. Using media other than language to express ideas (e.g., does not use pictures, etc., when appropriate to express ideas; does not use aesthetic forms such as dance-drama to express ideas)

2. Understanding the ideas of others
   a. Reading (e.g., has not developed visual or auditory discrimination; makes errors; reads haltingly; repeats words; lacks knowledge and/or confidence in word-attacking skills; unable to distinguish difference between similar words; unable to remember new words learned; does not comprehend material; does not read for fun or information; does not know left and right; unable to remember what is read; lacks sufficient background of experience to understand words and simple ideas)
   b. Listening (e.g., does not remember oral instructions; does not appear to hear what is said; misinterprets what he is told; is inattentive, unable to concentrate; does not evaluate informal discussions, conversation, or oral presentations; is not interested in musical and dramatic forms of expression)
   c. Observing (e.g., does not observe or is not aware of environmental surroundings; cannot interpret environmental surroundings; does not remember visual symbols; can't focus eyes on object while head is moving; has mannerisms that indicate he has trouble seeing)

3. Dealing with quantitative relationships
   a. Interpreting number values and symbols (e.g., does not understand meaning of symbols; confuses serial order of numbers; does not know number names; does not know number processes; cannot

visualize special concepts; cannot hold math concepts; has little understanding of quantitative terms —large, small, tall, short; misunderstands locational terms—on, over, in, etc.; no concept of the use of zeros)

b. Use of number in context (e.g., cannot understand transportation schedules, house numbers, charts, maps, thermometer; cannot find page by number, dial a telephone, keep score; cannot read calendar; has no understanding of savings and checking accounts)

c. Fractions and decimals (e.g., has no concept of fractions or decimals)

d. Geometry (e.g., cannot visualize shapes and forms)

e. Computation and problem-solving (e.g., cannot estimate amounts; cannot make exact computations)

f. Use of units and instruments of measure (e.g., does not understand or use units of measure; cannot use measuring instruments)

g. Time (e.g., is not aware of time; cannot tell time)

h. Money (e.g., does not know value of units of change; cannot make change)

4. Using effective methods of work

a. Planning (e.g., is not organized; does not plan ahead; cannot decide on goal or purpose; destroys work for little if any cause; cannot set up hypothesis; cannot determine sequence of steps to achieve purpose; is unable to budget time and energy; is unable to evaluate steps taken)

b. Using appropriate resources (e.g., does not know where to locate pertinent resources; cannot evaluate resources; wastes resources)

c. Use of scientific approach for the study of situations (e.g., does not use problem-solving approach to practical problems; superstition guides some behavior)

C. Problem in Moral Choices—Values

1. Determining the nature and extent of individual freedom
   a. Responding to authority (e.g., does not cooperate in enforcing regulations; does not feel obligated to follow rules laid down by constituted authority; comes late; resents any rule; negative reaction to group mores; goes against traditions which hinder him; cheats)
   b. Acting upon a personal set of values (e.g., does not have a set of values which hinder himself and others, won't stand up for own point of view)

2. Determining responsibility to self and others
   a. Preserving integrity in human relationships (e.g., does not carry out commitments; has no respect for property rights—borrows without permission, steals; is not honest)
   b. Meeting the needs of others (e.g., is not aware of individual differences; is usually unwilling to modify personal desires in the interests of others; does not share)
   c. Developing and using potential abilities of self and others (e.g., has no desire to develop individual capacities and social ends; does not seek or secure contributions of all concerned with a problem)

D. Problem in Achieving Aesthetic Expression and Appreciation

1. Expressing the self through varied media (e.g., does not use his own resources for aesthetic expression; does not experiment with varied media; has not developed special interests and abilities)

2. Achieving artistry in daily work (e.g., has no means of creative expression in work)

3. Achieving attractive personal appearance (e.g., is not aware of the need for good grooming; is not well

groomed; has poor manners; has poor posture—sitting, walking or standing; wears inappropriate clothing)

II. Situations Calling for Growth in Social Participation

A. Problems in Establishing Sound Person-to-Person Relationships

1. Establishing effective social relationships with others
   a. Developing friendships and affectionate relationships (e.g., has not developed affectionate relationships with family members; has not made good friends; does not seem aware of what it takes to make friends; abuses friendships; does not do things to show he is concerned about his friends and classmates; aggressive toward other children—bullies; hurts others; displays attention-getting behavior— throws things, tattles, teases; is not chosen as a partner; critical of other children's differences and/ or behavior; does not use courteous expressions; interrupts others when they are talking; makes unpleasant remarks during lunch)
   b. Participating in social and sports activities (e.g., does not use proper behavior during social or sports activities; does not follow rules of the game; does not accept role in planning or carrying out activity; has very little variety in his choice of activity; does not know what to do with leisure time)

2. Establishing effective working relations with others
   a. Working on a common enterprise (e.g., does not consider needs of others; takes on roles he cannot handle; insists on running project all the time; evades responsibility)

B. Group Membership

1. Deciding when to join a group
   a. Deciding when and how much group activity is desirable (e.g., has no basis for deciding what existing

groups to join; does not accept membership obligations; is not aware of proper relationship to be
maintained between group members)

2. Participating as a group member
    a. Helping to formulate group policy—rules (e.g., does
       not express opinions regarding group activity;
       overwhelms the group with his opinions and de-
       sires regarding group activity; will not agree to join
       in decisions; erratic behavior in deciding when to
       support organized group action, inappropriate
       suggestions)
    b. Selecting leaders (e.g., not aware of abilities and
       qualities needed by leaders; uses inappropriate
       evidence in choosing leaders)
    c. Helping carry out group responsibilities and poli-
       cies (e.g., does not evaluate the work of those to
       whom responsibility is delegated; does not assist
       in the execution of group decisions; gives little or
       no help in completion of procedures—does not
       clean up, is not dependable)

3. Taking leadership responsibilities
    a. Outlining preliminary plans (e.g., does not think
       ahead and plan for activities, needed personnel and
       materials)
    b. Securing participation of group members (e.g., uses
       poor or improper techniques in attempting to se-
       cure cooperative action)

C. Intergroup Relationships

1. Working with racial, religious and national groups
    a. Understanding and accepting the difference be-
       tween groups (e.g., uses unreliable or little infor-
       mation to form opinions of other groups; uses
       abusive language or action toward other groups)
    b. Safeguarding rights and responsibilities of racial,
       religious and national groups (e.g., is not aware of
       legal and personal obligations to racial, religious

and national groups; does not support legal and personal obligations to racial, religious and national groups)

D. School Activities

1. Accepting school as an integral, important part of life
   a. Understands the need for participating in schools (e.g., sees no value in school; dislikes school; refuses to participate in school activities; is truant)

III. Situations Calling for Growth in Ability to Deal with Environmental Factors and Forces

A. Natural Phenomena

1. Dealing with physical phenomena
   a. Adjusting to atmospheric conditions (e.g., does not wear clothing proper for weather conditions; is not aware of poor physical conditions in relation to light, air, heat, etc.)

B. Technological Resources

1. Using technological resources
   a. Using tools, machines and equipment (e.g., is unable to use common tools; does not know which tools and machines are used in various trades)
   b. Using household and office appliances (e.g., does not know the use of household appliances; does not use appropriate equipment to conserve human energy)
   c. Using instruments of communication (e.g., does not know how to use telephone effectively)
   d. Using transportation (e.g., does not know how to use bus transportation, trains; cannot read schedules)

C. Economic-Social-Political Structures and Forces

1. Earning a living
   a. Providing for work needs of society (e.g., will not

accept responsibility to aid society; is unable to decide what work to do)

b. Achieving effective workmanship (e.g., does not have adequate work standards; is not aware of what good working conditions are)

c. Assuring the rights and responsibilities of workers (e.g., has little idea of what is considered adequate remuneration)

d. Managing money (e.g., has no concept of budgeting income; has no savings or investing plan; does not realize the implications of borrowing money)

2. Securing goods and services

a. Buying and selling goods and services (e.g., has no logical basis for deciding where to buy or sell; has little awareness of how to determine quality; does not know how a fair price is determined)

3. Providing for social welfare

a. Working in the family group (e.g., does not have good relations with family members; does not share family responsibilities)

b. Participating in community welfare provisions (e.g., does not know how charitable organizations work; does not contribute to or work for charitable organizations)

c. Using government and other community agencies and services when appropriate (e.g., does not know about community agencies; does not know where to go in emergencies)

d. Using natural resources intelligently (e.g., wastes water and other resources)

CHAPTER 5

Problems That May Interfere
with Learning

The growth and development of children occurs in such an obvious manner, and we are often so close to the child, that we do not recognize how marvelously complex and inter-related these patterns are. If we are observant, we can see not only the physical growth but the great changes in every other human characteristic. The child broadens his horizons, de-velops new relationships, increases his strength, improves his motor skills and specialization of muscles, grows in his ability to think abstractly and solve problems, achieves greater skill in use of language and communications, develops new activi-ties, attitudes and interests, and becomes responsible as a more mature human being.

Growth and development is continuous but uneven. To assume that all children of a certain age must achieve a cer-tain standard belies the evidence that shows such a great range of development at any given age. Too frequently, the adult who sees one mature pattern erroneously assumes that all the others have achieved the same level of development. Observation of a rather sophisticated twelve-year-old boy breaking down and crying after losing a baseball game or being harassed by others is an example of uneven growth.

When the child arrives at school, he does not come with a clean slate ready to be written upon. Instead, he brings with him his own unique physical, social, emotional and intellectual level of development. These levels of development vary from child to child and are uneven in relationship to each other and influence the behavior of the child.

The child brings all his past experiences with him; he brings his relationships with his family, his friends and his neighborhood, since he is the product of having interacted with them. He has developed attitudes and values and has begun to develop his own view of the world. When we evaluate his readiness for performance in different areas of school activities, we must consider all these factors.

It is important that the teacher understand the general range of behavior that can be expected from children at various ages. Is there something wrong with six-year-old Janice because she flits from idea to idea, or do six-year-olds ordinarily behave this way? Does five-year-old Billy have a speech problem if he cannot say certain speech sounds? Does the fact that seven-year-old Paul stares out the window indicate a serious emotional problem? How does the teacher determine which are acceptable learning problems and behavior and which should be considered problems for which he requires help?

Behavior is a continuum; that is, there is no clean cut-off point at which the teacher can decide that certain patterns of growth or development do not fall into the normal range. Many other factors play important roles. It is essential for the teacher to know the sequence of development and the level which is required for each skill and area of performance in school. The skilled, trained teacher learns to know and accept each child and continually observes his behavior, in order to determine whether the child needs special assistance.

At first, the consequences of heredity and the faults in the environment affect the biological development of the embryo. Inborn errors may cause a lag in the development of some organ, and this problem in turn has an effect on the development of the rest of the body and may produce a general defect. An extended period of negative environmental conditions may cause the same type of problem. If they are serious enough, these biological defects will affect the physical or psychological development of the child as he grows and develops and cause problems in the future.

At the next level, certain environmental conditions may not be available to the child to stimulate him to develop his verbal abilities during the time this particular task should be learned. Some evidence regarding children from homes in low-income neighborhoods indicates that this lack of development frequently causes learning problems in school.[25]

As there is no single description of a child with a learning problem, there is no single cause for learning problems. Children with problems which prevent them from learning are those who may lack motivation, have poor eye control, are clumsy and heavy, inattentive, hyperactive, withdrawn, do work that is sloppy, write illegibly, have speech difficulties, poor coordination, and many others. With so many complicated problems, there are also a large number of interrelated causes. This discussion can only highlight the main causes. If the problem is serious, the teacher must call upon staff members with more specific training for more information.

A problem may have one cause or it may have several causes. The cause may be detected easily or it may be quite remote and unfathomable due to our present lack of specific knowledge in many areas. Our ability to identify the causes of problems that children have in school has increased tremendously during the last few years. A great deal has been learned about how we may prevent some of the conditions

[25] See, for example, Benjamin Bloom, *Stability and Change in Human Characteristics* (New York, John Wiley & Sons, 1964) and J. McV. Hunt, *Intelligence and Experience* (New York, Ronald Press, 1961).

which later cause children to have problems. Studies have identified the groups of students who are most susceptible to the kind of damage which can cause defects in growth and learning.

It is extremely important for the researchers to continue to spend a great deal of time and effort identifying specific causes. We find, however, that educators frequently spend a great deal of time discussing how to categorize children based on causes and/or the type of behavior they observe. While the cause for behavior *may* help determine the specific program technique, *it frequently plays no role.* In many cases, an evaluation of the present function of the child can provide us with sufficient information so that his specific program can be planned without knowing the specific cause.

As we study the literature related to the etiology of various conditions which cause learning problems, we cannot help but be astonished at the amazing consistency of the descriptions of the behavior of children who have different labels. Authors who use such designations as mental retardation, minimal brain injury, social and emotional handicaps, etc., refer to the same prenatal, paranatal and postnatal causes, to endogenous and exogenous causes, to heredity and environment, etc. As we describe the general causes of learning problems, we could easily and arbitrarily use almost any classification label as the title of the discussion. Even more remarkable is the finding that the same causes are suggested as the reasons for a wide variety of school related problems. For example, any reading text will explain, "Reading problems may be caused by physical, emotional, social or intellectual factors," and then go on to specific statements. The same statements may be found in books discussing the causes of problems in hearing and speech, under such labels as mental retardation, social-emotional handicaps, brain-injured, etc.

The specific causes of a problem that interferes with learning may occur at any time after the child is conceived. There may be damage to the embryo before birth or during birth. The causes may be so varied and so complicated that they are in the domain of individuals with rather specialized training. If we see development as continuous, then any problem that occurs at any time will cause a reaction and the organism will immediately begin to function in a different manner. As the child grows, the reaction may become more serious and complicated.

The problem of identifying specific causes continues to be a difficult one. Since behavior is influenced by a large number of factors, it is frequently impossible to isolate a single one. In many instances, a problem is caused by a situation which may, in itself, be caused by another factor. A child may refuse to participate in a discussion because children make fun of him because he has a speech impediment, which may have been caused by a birth injury. The teacher must work with the child and his classmates on a number of levels at the same time. The child must have a thorough medical and speech diagnosis and assistance as necessary. The child who has a problem must be accepted by the teacher, who in turn influences the other children to do the same. In addition, the teacher may encourage the youngster in areas of his own interest so that he meets with personal success and gains acceptance by the others, in order to overcome his refusal to participate.

Thus, any list of causes for certain behavior can only suggest a starting point from which the teacher may gain insight into the total behavioral and physical mechanisms which are at the root of the learning problem.

However, in order to give a general description of how school problems may be caused, we will discuss them in rather arbitrarily chosen and sometimes overlapping categories. The two general areas are problems which originate within the child and those which occur because of environmental conditions. Since behavior is a function of the interaction of the individual in his environment, such a separation can be justified only to simplify our discussion. The following outline is used because it represents a simplified method for the teacher to use to check the possible causes. Each act of behavior is a result of all the previous experiences the child brings, the variables related to the present task and his motives for the future. Obviously, any attempt to organize these causes must be oversimplified, as they are in the following list, since many are interrelated and inseparable. Keeping the complicated nature of behavior in mind, the author has discussed each cause or group of causes to emphasize its importance and possible contribution to the problem.

The following outline lists a wide variety of variables which may cause children to fail to reach the goals set by the school and the teacher. The discussions of the particular variables are given on the pages listed in parentheses. The outline may also be used as a checklist to analyze a particular problem.

Outline of Factors
Which May Cause Child
to Fail to Reach School Goals

I. Task, Method or Experience Variables

    A. Problems related to task or method (see Chapters 2 and 3)

        1. Task too difficult; does not know what to do; has not mastered previous skills
        2. Task too lengthy
        3. Material has no meaning to child; does not see its purpose; uninteresting; child not involved in its choice
        4. Insufficient interesting practice
        5. Method unvaried, uninteresting; method does not appeal to all the senses

6. Teacher is not really interested or does not think material is important
7. Child has frequently failed same or similar tasks

B. Problems related to experiences (see page 96 in this chapter)

1. Child has had lack of specific experience and opportunity for:
   a. Verbal learning, conversation, language usage, listening
   b. Physical activity and development
   c. Functioning independently
   d. Playing with other children
   e. Learning appropriate, expected or required behavior—responses, eating habits, cleaning up, going to a theater
   f. Choosing and using relaxing and social activities—camping, picnicking
   g. Concept formation
   h. Cultural activities
   i. Variety of community experiences—stores, theaters
   j. Problem-solving behavior

2. Child has had negative experience and thus learned behavior which is inappropriate—adults are punishing and rejecting and not to be trusted, might makes right, only "sissies" do well in school, the world is a hostile place.

3. Child had different cultural experience (recent arrival from a foreign country, etc.)

II. Teacher Variables (see Chapter 2)

A. Poor teacher-pupil relations, when teacher:

1. Rejects children, dislikes them
2. Acts in punitive manner
3. Uses marks as weapons
4. Is unable to establish relationship with children

    5. Is overly rigid or overly permissive
    6. Teases or mocks children
    7. Stresses being perfect, is interested only in the best students

B. Teacher's failure as a person when he:
    1. Is tense, anxious, fearful
    2. Feels he knows it all and children must listen
    3. Rejects outside assistance
    4. Insists that all problems stem from outside the classroom
    5. "Never" has a problem with a child
    6. Has a poor self-image, frequently runs himself down
    7. Is lazy, works only when children are in room, does not correct all papers, uses only material from book
    8. Is more interested in how he looks to others than in the children
    9. Is waiting to retire
    10. Has outside responsibilities that are too heavy a burden, so that he is not able to devote enough time and energy to teaching
    11. Does not fight for what he thinks is right

C. Teacher's lack of technical skills, when he:

    1. Does not use best principles of psychology in teaching
    2. Does not know child development
    3. Is not oriented to individual children
    4. Is too rigid or uncreative to be able to deal with children's varied needs and interests
    5. Chooses inappropriate goals
    6. Does not use effective thinking or problem-solving in his approach to teaching, nor does he set a good example for the children

III. Individual Variables

    A. Physical problems due to damage affecting the brain or central nervous system (see page 112), involving:

1. Vision perception
2. Hearing perception
3. Speech
4. Motor sequences, balance, coordination
5. Memory
6. Emotional behavior, concentration
7. Height or weight

B. Physical problems due to damage affecting other parts of the body

1. Muscles or bones
2. Vision
3. Speech
4. Hearing
5. Medical

C. Problems in emotional-social behavior (see page 123) due to:

1. The child's negative or inappropriate self-image—insecure, anxious, with little self-confidence, or not aware of real strengths and weaknesses
2. Poor home situation
3. Traumatic experience—loss of parent, serious accident, etc.
4. Frequent failure
5. Teacher's immature behavior—hostile, overprotective, etc.
6. Serious physical handicap.

IV. School and Community Variables (see page 131)

A. Insufficient pupil personnel services; little help available to teacher for evaluation of children and program suggestions; poor organization of services; poor communication among staff members; little relationship to other community agencies

B. Inadequate or untrained supervision

C. Poor physical facilities and surroundings
1. Physical surroundings in school—poor equipment or lighting, inadequate space
2. Poor home conditions—poor living space; poor diet; lack of equipment, books, toys; lack of routine eating and sleeping
3. Community facilities—inadequate library facilities, museums

D. Inappropriate general school programs and goals set for children; all children must meet same requirements, etc.

E. Poor family situation

1. Parents: rejecting; overprotecting; rigid; permissive; divorced, separated, or deceased; emotional problem; lack of attention and care; too many siblings; serious illness; too much pressure to do well; poor opinion of teachers and/or school
2. Siblings: emotional problems; poor relationship; too many children; competing; older child must take responsibility for younger ones; heavy burden of responsibility

I. Task, Method or Experience Variables

A. *Problems Related to Task or Method:* When the teacher has described the behavior of the child in an objective manner and has stated the specific goal for the task or activity which the child was to perform, he then analyzes the task assigned and the method used to determine if these are appropriate. A thorough discussion of the evaluation procedure for determining the achievement level of each child appears in Chapter 3. The checklist on the previous pages suggests areas of variability to be considered in the teacher's examination of the task and the method.

B. *Problems Related to Experience:* There are many children who have problems which prevent them from learning who have no measurable physical or neurological symptomology. Until recently, they had not been identified until they failed in school situations or exhibited antisocial behavior.

Child-rearing practices and children's experiences have a tremendous impact on their mental and physical development. The deleterious effects of institutional care on the intellectual and emotional development of infants have been reported in many studies.[26]

It appears that inadequate degrees of sensory stimulation in the early life of a child decrease the activity of the reticular formation, which acts as an arousal agent, alerting the cortex, thus providing indispensable facilitation for perception, learning and motor activity. Thus, inadequate stimulation and experience can result in retarded intellectual and sensory-motor development, as can damage to the brain, which may interfere with the reception, transmission or cortical utilization of stimuli. There appear to be a number of "critical periods" of development during which perceptual stimulation seems to have the greatest long-range effectiveness.

One can conclude that there are multiple experiences a child must have in order to learn the skills required to successfully accomplish each stage of development and move on to the next. The lack of these experiences in the early years of life may later produce character and personality disorders and may impair the development of normal functioning.

A child who does not have a constant close relation-

[26] Seymour B. Sarason, *Psychological Problems in Mental Deficiency* (New York, Harper & Brothers, 1949), Chapter 6.

ship with his mother, which gives him affection and warmth, may develop a number of problems. Parents may not respond to the child's actions and stimulate and reinforce new behavior. Children may not be attended to when they are ill or uncomfortable, so that they face extended periods of both physical and emotional frustration and deprivation.

There are a great many factors which cause the child to develop a poor self-image or to slow down development in physical or mental growth and learning.

Although poverty alone does not produce these results, patterns which may have this result are more common in certain segments of the lower socioeconomic groups and perpetuate it from one generation to another. By the time many of these children reach nursery school, certain patterns which prevent the child from learning have already been established. *Early intervention is indicated.*

For[27] too long a time we have been satisfied with thinking theoretically and have failed to act. If we do not change, we are using our educational system to doom another generation of these children to failure. The following are considerations in planning programs and instruction for pupils with disadvantaged backgrounds. These are the thoughts of those who have studied, worked and lived with these children. The goal must be an improved educational program, one that will result in breaking the vicious poverty cycle.

It is absolutely essential to understand that these

[27] The following material on the so-called culturally disadvantaged, previously written by the author, has appeared in *The Connecticut Teacher,* March 1966.

considerations are not to be regarded as characteristic of all children who come from homes located in neighborhoods which house families whose income is low. To do so would be to disregard individual differences and to infer a homogeneity that does *not* exist. These children are as different from one another as are children in any other group. Each child must be evaluated to determine his specific needs in planning a program for him.

These are general considerations for children whose early lives lack certain necessary stimulation, experiences and relationships. No *one* statement applies to all such children and no *one* child's function is such that it can fit all of the considerations. In the cities these apply to ghettoized Negroes and those of Puerto Rican origin. In rural areas, their application may be more general.

The first and most important initial goal is to help these children learn to *like* school and all that is associated with it, to trust the teacher, to feel secure and accepted in the class. *This is to be accomplished without being concerned about whether or not they learn traditional subjects or learn them in the usual manner.*

1. Cultural milieu

   a. If they are American Negroes, they are frequently sensitive about their skin color because of the way society has treated them. If they are Americans of Puerto Rican origin, they are proud of their origin but resentful of society's general rejection of them. If they are others who live in poverty, they are also involved in a vicious cycle, including lack of education and job opportunities, which has perpetuated this rather hopeless existence.

b. They may live with physical aggression ("might makes right"), disease, worry, fear of separation, fear of eviction, fear of homelessness, fear of hunger, broken homes, fear of family resentment for not contributing financially.

c. They may live in a world they have come to consider rather hopeless and may not be protected from the crises of life. They may sit with the ill and the dying and listen to talk of unemployment and marital troubles. They hear talk of being an unwanted child ("what we could have done if it weren't for Johnny").

d. They may belong to a family with characteristics which include: Cooperativeness and mutual aid; avoidance of competition; freedom from self-blame; freedom from parental overprotection; children's enjoyment of each other's company; lessened sibling rivalry; no real sense of security; enjoyment of games and cars; the ability to express anger; a physical style of reacting.

e. Pupils and parents may be "anti-intellectual" (not anti-education). They may not like middle-class, thinking people (who have failed to help them improve their situation) but they frequently accept the importance of education.

f. They probably do not understand how the middle class lives and thinks.

g. They may not have developed habits of planning and thinking out a problem but tend to attack it directly.

h. Their view of the "outside" world is frequently grossly distorted and is the result of seeing it through TV, films and other very limited experiences.

i. Boys and girls usually have not been helped to assess their skills.

j. Their family constellations are frequently not the same as that of a middle-class family. It may consist of a mother and the children and other relatives; a grandmother; or a number of other compositions; not necessarily father, mother and children.

k. Their peer group has an extremely high priority as a determinant of their actions.

l. Boys and girls are concerned with and focused on trouble, toughness, endurance, "outsmarting the other guys"; fate and luck; desire for independence (while feeling alone and needing someone to depend upon), and for excitement as a means of escape from the boredom of their everyday lives.

m. They appear to be conscious of "right and wrong" and the rules of society; although they frequently violate them, it is sometimes because of lack of understanding. In spite of their unusual amount of norm-violating behavior, they frequently make choices which keep them out of trouble.

n. The basis for prestige, which is extremely important to them, is frequently their bravery, fearlessness, toughness, physical prowess, ability to "con" people; smart repartee, seeking and finding thrills, danger, and defying authority.

o. There is a great deal of pressure on children to leave school. Their peers may taunt them and tag them as effeminate, and their families frequently ask for their financial assistance. If they want to continue their education, they are very often emotionally in conflict with their environment.

p. They often have been deprived of verbal stimulation. Adults around them may not really talk with them. They may never have heard a bedtime story. They frequently feel that those who have made it into the middle class have deserted them.

2. Personal attributes

a. They are more like their more normal peers than not.

b. They grow up faster. They live in a society where they are expected to act as men or women by age thirteen or fourteen. (Sometimes younger, depending on family setup.)

c. Boys act in terms of their concept of being more male (coarser, more aggressive physically, more open sexually, use of profanity) than the average boy from a family having an average or above-average income. Girls attempting to act more adult are often bolder, are aware of sex, related experiences and references at an early age.

d. They usually have strong intergroup loyalty.

e. They can frequently function quite well in an informal structure.

f. They often have a good sense of humor.

g. They usually thrive on respect.

h. The children are quite frequently emotional and they tend to be noisy when happy. No disrespect is intended when the group gets loud.

3. Attitudes toward education and teachers

    a. Children and their parents have a much more positive attitude toward education than is generally believed. They have a feeling that somehow education may help them out of the closed poverty cycle in which they live.

    b. However, they may dislike school because they are often treated as second-class citizens.

    c. They often face discrimination because of their lack of experience and the school's preset conditions.

    d. They have a great deal of fear of being overpowered by teachers in situations where they do not accept the teacher's point of view.

    e. Pupils with disadvantaged backgrounds have a sixth sense about how people feel about them. They report that they can feel when the teacher does not like them as soon as they walk into a room.

    f. Parents and pupils have been more responsive to, and more involved in, schools which have demonstrated concern for their ideas, aspirations and problems.

4. Educational deficits

    a. They are usually not set to respond to oral or written stimuli.

    b. Their auditory attention set is not often well developed, so they have trouble listening.

    c. Their time perspective is often different when compared to that of the middle- or high-income group. Time for eating and sleeping is not set and may vary from day to day.

d. They often have limited experience with formal language. As a result, people sometimes wrongly think they are nonverbal.

e. They appear to be relatively slow in performing intellectual tasks, not because they are dull, but because they have not learned to generalize easily.

f. They may have difficulty understanding a concept unless they actually have something to do which shows what it means in some direct, concrete matter.

g. They may not have learned how to get a job, prepare for an interview, fill out a form, take tests and answer questions.

h. They may have difficulty with spatial relationships, so that they may have trouble with numerical or geometric concepts.

5. Educational strengths

a. Deprived pupils are often very persistent about something when they develop an interest in it.

b. They can be quite articulate in conversation with people whom they trust and with whom they feel comfortable about subjects they know about.

c. They are often surprisingly articulate in role-playing situations.

d. They usually have hidden verbal ability.

6. Learning modes

a. They may be physical learners, rather than oral.

b. They respond most readily to visual and kinesthetic signals.

c. They are often content-centered rather than form-centered, externally oriented rather than introspective, and problem-centered rather than abstract-centered.

d. They can be taught adult behavior if they follow the teacher's example. That is, they need strong, well-adjusted adult models.

e. They have more trouble thinking the way a teacher does than do children from the middle-economic-class home.

f. If teachers act toward them in a manner indicating they think they are dull, the children frequently behave as if they are dull.

g. They may learn language better through speech rather than reading. Discussions teach them sentence patterns. They may talk in what is termed a "swinging" manner only because they don't want to be called "squares."

h. They generally need more practice in language-readiness programs. Language laboratories and storytelling will help.

i. While they have trouble with school word games, they apparently do quite well with word games they learn in their neighborhood. Rhythm may play a key role.

j. They sometimes cannot learn language through rules or through drills on other people's sentences.

k. Teachers must observe the following principles:

    i. All learning is stimulated or hindered by the teacher's feelings toward the pupil.

    ii. All learning is influenced by how close the curriculum comes to the child's personal life and concerns.

l. At first these pupils will generally learn by utilizing one track at a time; that is, they persist in one line of thought, rather than try to handle multiple considerations.

m. They need immediate reinforcement. The teacher must pick up what they say, appeal to them and pitch examples to them.

n. Some live for today. Reward must be immediate.

o. They need more varied experiences than their circumscribed life affords. They need field trips, including visits to factories, terminals, new neighborhoods, museums, concerts and theaters.

p. They frequently need additional practice in work of the pre-first-grade level.

q. They need a great deal of individual attention.

r. Writing assignments should be unstructured, associative. Subjects which are middle-economic-class-oriented are often a waste of time and set up negative responses.

s. In assigning writing activities, teachers should make a much closer analysis of the relationship of writing errors to speech, make much more use of speaking as a device for improvement of writing.

t. Pupils frequently see reading as a school activity only. Teachers must help them realize that reading can be a normal, agreeable part of both school and home life.

u. They should have literature and reading that shows that everyone can fail, has problems, can have his dignity shattered, is frightened, has enemies, etc., but that these problems are frequently overcome.

v. The learning principle which recommends proceeding from experience to speaking, to writing, to reading, is of critical importance for them.

w. Their reality is their environment. Their school books must come reasonably close to that environment, or they may feel that we are telling them that we do not consider their lives worthwhile.

x. They divide people into "in-group" and "outsiders." Stealing from "outsiders" is okay as long as they get away with it. However, taking things from the "in-group" is unacceptable behavior.

7. Classroom procedures

a. The problem is first one of achieving classroom rapport. The teacher must truly respect and accept these children as worthwhile individuals. He cannot be naive or foolish or soft. He can expect a difficult initial period and that his acceptance by the children will come slowly.

b. Rules regarding fighting and destruction of property must be effected early and carried out consistently.

c. These children have usually had little experience in listening to adults talk for long periods of time and cannot concentrate in this type of situation. Don't talk constantly but work on developing an "auditory set."

d. A carefully detailed plan to help the children understand the school's "set" must be initiated and carried out, starting on the first day.

e. Role playing is extremely important in helping the teacher's understanding of situations.

f. Fear of failure plays a dominant role in the youngster's reaction to his activities in school.

Material must be on their level and constant reaffirmation of ability must be given. At first, the topics discussed with these children should be those that *they* choose as the ones in which they are interested. Later on, other topics can be introduced by the teacher. These, then, may lead to the third level, which is learning for its own sake.

g. The teacher's strength can be displayed to these children by definiteness, quiet, firm tones, consistency, standing by a statement, determination to teach, and so on, without being negative and rigid. It is a serious mistake to think and to function as though authority and respect can be commanded by physical power alone.

h. Pictures of Negro and Puerto Rican doctors, nuclear physicists, journalists, and other people who have risen from poverty to become successful should be displayed in the classrooms to suggest higher horizons, to instill motivation, and improve the child's self-image.

i. Children need to be prepared well in advance for all the trips and events that take place with full explanations, pictures, etc. Without full preparation, they lose most of their value.

j. Classrooms and libraries should be open during after-school hours, giving children who come from crowded, noisy homes the opportunity for quiet study. Teachers should be available for help.

k. Plays and stories are much more interesting when they can be carefully selected in terms of the existing cultural interests of these groups.

l. The children may lack important test-taking skills, have had insufficient practice, and have little motivation. There may be an absence of rapport with the examiner who has different values. (It was demonstrated that when these areas were improved, children improved enormously on standard tests, despite the cultural bias of these instruments.)

m. Games are a good technique for teaching and also for discovering the level of function of children, since they are usually highly motivated during this type of activity.

n. A reading program with experiences dealing more directly with people and events arouses sympathy, curiosity and wonder in these children. Texts which recognize the building of values should be used.

o. A basic, stimulating structure, combined with emphasis on physical learning, probably will be most effective. The present, highly competitive system of marks, exams and comparisons of all sorts should be replaced by other types of incentives to learning. Marks and grades hurt more than they help. They discourage students from studying hard subjects and from electing good but tough teachers.

p. Intramural activities should be encouraged and planned.

q. The library should be a focal point of the school, attractive, easy to use, accessible to students at all times; and continuing instruction should be given in library use for research and general reading purposes. A wide variety of books must be available.

r. Habits of study and learning should be emphasized and encouraged.

s. Imagination helps children get more out of their rather narrow existence. Teachers must work to stimulate and encourage children to try out new ideas. A questioning attitude must be reinforced and developed. Children enjoy playing such games as "How would I change the world?" and "If I had three wishes," and teachers can learn a great deal about their children from their responses.

t. Holidays, birthday parties, etc., should be emphasized. A party for each child should be planned. Members of the family should be invited to the birthday parties.

u. Children should be encouraged to care for small pets and learn to be responsible for them.

v. The presence of Negro and Puerto Rican professionals in the school or during trips is especially important.

w. Nutrition appears to play an important role in preparing the children for continued learning activity. Each child's eating habits can be improved and provision may be made by the school for a lunch or breakfast program if necessary.

If teachers cannot change their style of teaching or if the school will not support such changes, then we will continue to use our education system to perpetuate the existing conditions.[28]

What it comes down to, as I tell the groups of teachers I work with, is that we must have very clearly in our minds what

28 Milton Young, "Planning Programs for the Disadvantaged." *Connecticut Teacher*, Connecticut Education Association, March 1966.

educational goals we have for these children. Should our goal be that these youngsters learn the important things in life: not to steal, not to hit people over the head, to be able to stand some small frustration and still go on with the task? Or should our goal be that they learn, like Lee Harvey Oswald, to read and write, no matter what?[29]

In summary, the inconsistent parent, the overly strict or permissive parent, the home that lacks effective relationships, the home that restricts the child's activity, all tend to produce patterns which interfere with the growth and learning potential of infants and young children. The removal or absence of the mother for extended periods of time, the lack of a father figure, the needs of other younger children may affect the child's concept of himself and his ability to relate to others as well as his concept of the world.

While there is no agreement as to the best rearing practices among those who study child growth and development, there is a great deal of consistency in statements regarding poor practices.

An additional complicating factor is discussed by Newell Kephart, who points out that: "The human organism is required to make more complex, more rapid adjustments than any other organism."[30] And, "He [the child] must not only respond to environmental changes as they occur but must also anticipate such changes and prepare his behavior ahead of time."[31]

[29] Bruno Bettelheim, "Teaching the Disadvantaged," *NEA Journal*, September 1965, p. 12.

[30] Newell C. Kephart, *The Slow Learner in the Classroom* (Columbus, Ohio, Charles E. Merrill Books, Inc., 1960) , p. 3.

[31] *Ibid.*, p. 6.

II. Teacher Variables

It would appear obvious that the teacher plays an extremely important role in helping the child when he appears unable to learn. Unfortunately, few teachers examine their own behavior when diagnosing a child's problem. Chapter 2 discusses the teacher's role in detail and suggests techniques for self-evaluation.

III. Individual Variables

A. *Physical problems due to damage affecting the brain or central nervous system:* Damage to the brain or central nervous system may or may not result in specific, identifiable symptoms. It may cause a number of conditions that occur singly or in combination. A great deal of confusion exists in education because of the various attempts to classify the dysfunctions caused by injury to the brain. It is worthwhile pointing out the importance of determining the nature of specific problems instead of spending an inordinate amount of time on assigning a label. The following quotations are examples of the uselessness of such labels in all areas of special legislation, since they define a great variety of behaviors and are therefore of no help to the teacher planning his procedure.

Cerebral palsy embraces the clinical picture created by injury to the brain, in which one of the components is motor disturbance. Thus, cerebral palsy may be described as a group of conditions, usually originating in childhood, characterized by paralysis, weakness, incoordination or any other aberration of motor function caused by pathology of the motor control center of the brain. In addition to such motor dysfunction, cerebral palsy may include learning difficulties, psychological problems, sensory defects, convulsive and behavioral disorders of organic origin.[32]

Wortis[33] tells us that "there is no brain-injured child," but rather a large number of children who may have some brain injury but whose behavior is as different from one another as it is from any other child. Disorganized behavior is one of the characteristics pointed out as suggestive of brain injury. However, other authors[34] are quick to point out that disorganized behavior does not always mean brain injury, nor does brain injury always mean disorganized behavior.

The following terms, plus many others, have been used to describe children with learning problems due to some suggested or actual damage to the brain or central nervous system:

Aggressive Behavior Disorder

Agnosia

Aphasia

Aphasic Syndrome

Apraxia

Association Deficit Pathology

Attention Disorders

Auditorially-Perceptually Impaired

Brain-Damaged

Brain-Injured

Central Nervous System Damage

Cerebral Dysfunction

Cerebral Dyssynchronization Syndrome

Cerebral Palsy

Character Impulse Disorder

Choreiform Syndrome

---

[32] The United Cerebral Palsy Research and Educational Foundation, *Program for Calendar Year 1958* (New York, The Foundation, 1958), p. 1.

[33] Joseph Wortis, "A Note on the Concept of the Brain Injured Child," *American Journal on Mental Deficiency,* 61:204–206, 1956.

[34] Seymour Sarason, *Psychological Problems in Mental Deficiency* (New York, Harper, 1949) and Herbert Buch, "Theoretical Aspects of Psychological Behavior in the Brain Damaged," *Psychological Services for the Cerebral Palsied,* by Morton Goldstein, United Cerebral Palsy Association, 1956, p. 56 ff.

Clumsy Child Syndrome
Conceptually Handi-
capped
Diffuse Brain Damage
Dysacousia
Dyslexia
Dyssynchronous
Hyperexcitability Syn-
drome
Hyperkinetic Behavior
Syndrome
Hyperkinetic Impulse
Disorder
Hyperkinetic Syndrome
Hypolinetic Syndrome
Interjacent Child
Learning Disabilities
Minimal Brain Damage
Minimal Brain Dysfunc-
tions
Minimal Brain Injury
Minimal Cerebral
Damage
Minimal Cerebral Injury
Minimal Cerebral Palsy

Minimal Chronic Brain
Syndrome
Minor Brain Damage
Neurologically Impaired
Organic Behavior Dis-
order
Organic Brain Damage
Organic Brain Disease
Organic Brain Dys-
function
Organic Driveness
Perceptual Cripple
Perceptually Handi-
capped
Primary Reading Re-
tardation
Psychoneurological
Learning Disorders
Scatter Child
Special Child
Specific Reading Dis-
ability
Strauss Syndrome
Visually-Perceptually
Impaired

Other labels can be added to this list, each attempting to describe a particular problem or syndrome but
frequently doing nothing more than adding to the
confusion that already exists in regard to planning
educational programs for children.

Injury to the brain may cause specific problems
in: *perception*—hearing, vision, kinesthesia; *concept
formation*—thinking, reasoning, memory; *motor behavior*—body movement, language, tumors, epilepsy;

or *emotional behavior,* which may be uneven or un-controllable. Any of these problems may occur either singly or in combination. Brain injury may also re-sult in disparity in growth, so that a child may have average development in one specific area of function and underdevelopment or defective development in another.

To add to the confusion, developmental anomalies may be caused by immaturity, slow development or long-term illness, as well as by injury to the brain, and these too may underlie physical problems in any of the areas affecting learning.

If a child shows indications of damage to the brain or central nervous system, he should be referred for a physical examination, since medical treatment, if any is possible, should always precede activities planned by the school to overcome these problems.

The general areas that can be checked to determine whether problems exist are: (1) *problems related to incoming stimuli:* hearing, seeing, tactile-kinesthetic; (2) *problems related to the brain itself:* understand-ing, remembering, retrieval; (3) *problems related to the output activities:* speaking, motor acts.

The activities that are suggested for the ameliora-tion of problems caused by injury are not specifically different from those for children who have not had certain necessary experiences. Newell Kephart[35] sug-gests that artificial means must be used to provide the necessary practice in perceptual motor skills, re-gardless of the origin of the problem.

In order for the teacher to determine the nature of the problem, a number of simple questions have been

[35] Newell C. Kephart, *The Slow Learner in the Classroom* (Columbus, Ohio, Charles E. Merrill Books, Inc., 1960) .

evolved. When a child deviates from the general age norms, the teacher's suspicion should be aroused. Serious discrepancies between expected and observed behavior should be referred for further evaluation.

The following are some of the questions the teacher must ask himself:

1. Can he hear me?

   Evaluation: All children should have their hearing tested when they enter school. If the teacher suspects there is a hearing problem, the child should be referred for testing.

2. Does he have a vision problem?

   Evaluation: As with hearing, each child should have a thorough vision testing. The Snellen Eye Chart is not sufficient for this purpose, and each school system must develop an adequate screening program.

3. Can the child learn through his tactile senses?

   Evaluation: Put a number of familiar items in a bag. Have the child reach in and pick out something. Have him describe it without looking at it.

4. Does the child understand what is is told or what he sees? (auditory and visual comprehension)

   Evaluation: This is a difficult area to measure since this measurement requires output of some kind. If the output areas (motor and speech) are injured, we cannot tell whether or not the child understands. If the child does not appear to have difficulty with speaking or motor activities but does not respond accurately to verbal, visual or tactile questions, he may have a problem comprehending the information coming into his brain. Have the child simply nod or point or say yes or no to verbal and picture or written directions.

5. Can the child remember what he hears? (auditory memory)

   Evaluation: Ask the child to respond either verbally or with motor actions to a sequence of instructions. Increase their complexity to check extent of memory.

6. Can the child remember what he sees? (visual memory)

   Evaluation: Show the child a series of objects on a table for one minute. Then cover them and ask him to name the objects. Increase the number and reduce observation time to checp further.

7. Can he retrieve the information he has learned when he needs it?

   Evaluation: Several days later, present the child with a problem which he has already solved easily. Can he retrieve the information?

8. Can the child give you an oral response to a visual and a spoken instruction? (visual-verbal and verbal-verbal)

   Evaluation: Have the child tell you what you are doing. Raise your hands, close your eyes, point your finger, etc. Ask the child to respond orally to questions you know he can answer. Do not let him see your mouth.

9. Can the child control his motor actions and respond to verbal and visual instructions? Check if distance is a factor. (verbal-motor and visual-motor)

   Evaluation: Play "Simple Simon Says" but do not not do any of the motions yourself. Or, have the child emulate your actions as you perform various motor tasks. Hands over your head, open your mouth, etc. (no verbal cues). Can the child copy designs or letters from the blackboard?

10. Can the child recognize similarities and differences among pictures and printed symbols? (vision perception)

    Evaluation: Have the child describe or point to the differences and similarities among pictures and symbols. Begin with simple material and move toward the more complex to establish the threshold. (Problems in motor coordination or speech may complicate this procedure.)

11. Can the child hear differences among sounds he hears?

    Evaluation: Have the child either reproduce sounds that you make, or indicate if they are different from one another or the same by a simple motor or verbal response.

12. Can the child conceptualize and hold abstract ideas?

    Evaluation: Have the child describe a procedure without using motions (e.g., how he puts his shirt on). Have him describe the similarities in a group or class (e.g., doors, what the common elements are that all doors have).

13. How long is the child's attention span?

    Evaluation: Check child when he is doing something he likes to do, something he is obviously interested in. Keep an accurate account of time with a watch.

14. Does the child know his right from his left, and has he developed laterality (right or left side)?

    Evaluation: Ask child to follow your actions as you stand beside him. Ask him to raise his right hand, stand on his left foot, reach with his left hand, etc.

    Make a cylinder of a piece of paper. Set it down in front of child. Ask him to look through it at something on other side of the room. If he hesitates to bring it up to one eye or the other, he may not have developed laterality.

Put objects on a table in front of child. Have him keep his hands at edge of table. At your signal, have him reach and bring one object in front of him. The hand he uses is his dominant hand. If he switches from hand to hand, he may not have developed handedness.

15. Does the child have gross motor coordination and control?
    Evaluation: Can the child skip, walk a narrow board, jump, hop, etc.? (Check ability as related to age.)
16. Has the child developed fine motor coordination?
    Evaluation: Can the child hold a pencil, speak fluently, color within lines, etc.?

The general classroom teacher who becomes familiar with the complex process of learning can try a number of activities suggested in the next chapter which can help the child with minimal problems. When he has exhausted the techniques he has at hand or when it is obvious that the child has a serious problem, he must seek the assistance of specialized personnel. When such specialists are unavailable, the teacher should study the literature to identify activities that may be helpful until he can get the help he needs. The bibliography at the end of the book suggests some of these resources.

B. *Physical problems due to damage affecting other parts of the body:* When a child deviates physically from what is expected for his age, he frequently encounters problems which prevent his learning. This problem may stem from the condition itself or from the reaction of others to it (e.g., children who have epileptic seizures).

Florence Goodenough[36] writes:

There is voluminous literature dealing with orthopedically handicapped groups of different etiologies; at present, there appears to be no good evidence that the cause of the crippling is of any great significance in determining the effects on the crippled child. The major factors in this respect seem to be: (1) the degree to which the crippling, after maximum correction by medical, surgical, and prosthetic devices, interferes with any particular pre-existing vocational aims (2) the attitude of the crippling prevalent among the child's immediate family and close associates (3) the attitude and overt reactions of the general public (4) the age at crippling, and (5) the personality of the crippled child.

The actual degree of crippling often seems less important than other factors.

A wide variety of problems stem from the condition itself. Some of these include:

1. "Orthopedic conditions [which] are those that interfere with the normal use of bones, muscles or joints. These conditions may be caused by 'infections' such as polio, congenital abnormalities such as clubfoot, traumatic crippling such as amputation resulting from accidents, tumors or cysts that disrupt the normal life process, atrophy, a wasting away of bones, spinal curvature or hunchback and more than seventy others."[37]

---

[36] Florence L. Goodenough, *Exceptional Children* (New York: Appleton-Century-Crofts, Inc., 1956), p. 389.

[37] William Cruckshank and Orville Johnson, *Psychology of Exceptional Children and Youth* (Englewood Cliffs, New Jersey, Prentice-Hall, 1958), p. 430.

2. A number of conditions affecting the eyes contribute to problems which prevent learning. The more common conditions include general refractive errors, a number of developmental abnormalities, specific muscle defects and a group of diseases. Farsightedness, nearsightedness, astigmatism, cross-eyedness, double vision, weak eyes, are examples of some of the more specific conditions.

3. Problems in speech or oral communication interfere with an individual's relationship to the world around him and to his interrelationship with others, and can also operate as a block to learning. A number of things can go wrong with speech. These include: (1) delayed or inadequate speech development, (2) "difficulty in producing the speech sounds accurately, correctly and clearly,"[38] and (3) inadequacy of tone, sound or fluency of the speech that is produced.

4. The child who has a condition that interferes with hearing faces serious problems in learning, since this avenue of communication can affect comprehension, speech, reading and writing. The seriousness of the problem depends upon: (1) the extent of the loss, (2) the age of onset, (3) acceptance of parents and their willingness to cooperate, (4) presence of other problems, and (5) comprehension.

5. A child may have missed a great deal of schoolwork because he has or has had a serious or chronic medical problem. Sometimes the illness or condition keeps him from or limits his participating in all of the school activities. The teacher must make every effort to provide a secure and

[38] *Ibid.*, p. 387.

accepting environment for a child whose medical condition causes him problems in learning.

Some children develop problems which are the result of the reaction of others to the condition. It would be erroneous to minimize the intensity of the feelings of a child and his parents regarding deviant conditions. There is a great deal of disappointment and emotional conflict, and the need for special treatment and other problems can be disastrous to the parent and the child.

Since all children have the same basic needs of love, success, friends and the same dreams, children with physical problems must be accepted and respected for themselves as individuals. They do not want pity. Yet, because of this special condition, they sometimes look different and can't do all the same things. Many such children face great emotional problems and need additional asistance to learn to live a happy life.

In too many instances the condition which may cause the child to have problems in some areas is not as great a barrier to self-acceptance as is other people's reaction to it. Frequently, people think of specific problems when they hear labels such as "deaf," "orthopedically handicapped" or "mentally retarded." They expect all such individuals to function similarly to each other. It is not easy to avoid this, since we tend to generalize about a great many concepts. The individuals who have a disabling condition vary from one to another as much as any other two people in the world. However, we frequently react to them in such a way as to inflict hardships and cause them to lack self-acceptance. The sequence occurs in this way: (1) Most people, including professionals, view the condition or its label with preconceived ideas, and this arouses expectations for behavior. (2) The viewers assign a certain value and role to the individual with the handicap, which devalue the individual because he is different (3) This view has a negative influence on the person's feeling about himself when he compares these expectations with those of others, since he accepts this outside judgment. (4) These expectations become part of his feelings about himself and give rise to the kind of behavior expected. This behavior tends to encourage similar reactions from others in the future. It appears reasonable to assume that in most instances emotional prob-lems do not stem from the condition itself but have been caused by the way the world views the problem.

C. *Problems in emotional-social behavior: A method for early detection*

As in the case in all areas, the causes of problems in emotional-social behavior are extremely complex. It is virtually impossible to identify a specific psychological base as the cause for a particular problem in behavior. Children do not come to school with a "clean slate." They have had several extremely important years of experience with members of their family and others in their community. A child's behavior is a result of his interaction with his family, his peers, his home and his playthings, the space as well as his reaction to and the freedom of action he has had, how he has been treated, etc.

Of all the factors which have an influence on so-cial-emotional behavior, the family makes the greatest single impact. The early relationships of the child with his parents and siblings and with others, the attitudes of his parents toward each other and to him, the parents' methods of rearing him, the availability of appropriate materials and experiences, and many other factors related to his home environment play important roles in determining the emotional-social behavior of the child.

Parents serve as models for children, who unknowingly emulate their parents' attitudes and behavior. The actions of the parents may serve to help the child grow or they may actually inhibit or distort the developing learning organism. Parental rejection, overprotection, rigidity, pressure, or a lack of attention and care can cause serious distortion in the child's concept of himself.

Parental attitudes and relations toward each other have an important influence on the child's concept of himself and the world. Quarreling, divorce or separation, domination, use of the child as a weapon, lack of confidence in the other parent, long-term physical or emotional illness—all are regarded as being important determinants of problems in social-emotional behavior.

It is now rather widely accepted that the community itself may contribute to the formation of behavior patterns. Children who are found to have problems usually show some form of unhappiness, discontent or unevenness in their development early in their lives. Samuel Kirk suggests that "behavior problems are the outcome of frustration resulting from the discrepancy between the child's capacity to behave and the requirements of the environment."[39]

Eli Bower,[40] in an excellent article, suggests that the concept of behavior which interefers with learning that "would be of greatest use to school person-

[39] Samuel Kirk, *Educating Exceptional Children* (Boston, Houghton Mifflin Co., 1962) , p. 336.
[40] Eli M. Bower, "The Emotionally Handicapped Child and the School," *Journal of Exceptional Children,* September 1959. Reprinted by permission.

nel would be one which is operationally related to the possibility of early detection and intervention in the school." Extensive portions of Bower's article are quoted here, since it suggests a simplified but clear approach to finding children with problems in social-emotional behavior. He continues to explain that behavior becomes a problem when the child does not appear to be able to make reasonable choices from the possible behaviors that are available to him. "To live is to make choices." When a child's choices become severely limited by emotional blocks, his behavior becomes a problem in learning.

"The reduction of possible behavioral alternatives serves to further reduce the individual's degrees of freedom in social and educational endeavors. In addition, this reduced maneuverability or inflexibility in a changing world of mobile peers and events increases his susceptibility to behavior difficulties and interpersonal friction." The child "is therefore circumscribed as one having a higher degree of vulnerability to behavior problems and one who, as an adult, will exhibit this vulnerability in general health problems, poor interpersonal relationships, inability to function sexually or economically, inability to profit from experience, or lead a happy life." He presents the following outline as a tool for the teacher to help him recognize a child with potential or existing emotional problems.

Significant Behavioral Deviations: In terms of their visibility in school they can be perceived as children who demonstrate one or more of the following characteristics to a marked extent and over a period of time:

1. An inability to learn which cannot be explained by intellectual, sensory or health factors.

An inability to learn is perhaps the single most significant characteristic of emotionally handicapped children in school. Such non-learning may be manifested as an inability to profit from experience as well as inability to master skill subjects. The non-learner seldom escapes recognition. Achievement tests often confirm what the teacher has long suspected. If all other possibilities have been ruled out, emotional conflicts or resistances can be ruled in.

2. An inability to build or maintain satisfactory interpersonal relationships with peers and teachers.

   It isn't just getting along with others that is significant here. Satisfactory interpersonal relations refer to factors such as demonstrating sympathy and warmth toward others, ability to stand alone when necessary, ability to have close friends, ability to be aggressively constructive and to enjoy working and playing with others as well as enjoying working and playing by oneself. In most instances, children who are unable to build or maintain satisfactory interpersonal relationships are most visible to their peers. Teachers are also able to identify such children after a period of observation.

3. Inappropriate types of behavior or feelings under normal conditions.

   Inappropriateness of behavior or feeling can often be sensed by the teacher and peer groups. "She acts funny" the peer group may say. The teacher may find some children reacting disproportionately to a simple command such as "Please take your seat." What is appropriate or inappropriate is best judged by the teacher using his professional training, his daily observation of the child, and his experience working and interacting with the appropriate behavior of large numbers of normal children.

4. A general pervasive mood of unhappiness or depression.

   Children who are unhappy most of the time may demonstrate such feelings in expressive play, art work, written composition or in discussion periods. They seldom smile and usually lack a *joie de vivre* in their curriculum or social relationships. In the middle or upper grades a self-inventory is usually helpful in confirming suspicions.

5. A tendency to develop illnesses, pains, or fears associated with personal or school problems.

This tendency is sometimes difficult to observe without the help of the school nurse and parent. Illness may be continually associated with school pressures or develop when a child's confidence in himself is under stress. In some cases, however, such illnesses or fears may not be apparent to the teacher, nurse or parent; peers, however, are often aware of children who are sick after tests or have headaches before recitations.

The significant characteristics indicating a need for closer scrutiny are inability to learn, unsatisfactory interpersonal relationships, inappropriate behavior, unhappiness, and illness. These characteristics can, of course, be said to be true of all children to some degree at different times. There seems to be little likelihood of bypassing the "how much is too much" question in any descriptive attempt at separating the more vulnerable from the less vulnerable child. A more satisfactory analysis can be made by assessing classes by some standardized process in which perceptions by teacher, peers and self can be combined.[41]

A note of caution must be suggested in screening for children with emotional problems that prevent learning. Sometimes the behavior that may suggest an emotional problem may actually be idiosyncratic behavior. The key to determining the difference is in analyzing the cause.

What kinds of observations about personality would be most helpful in making inferences or professional guesses as to cause of deviant behavior? To the teacher or principal the behavior of the . . . child will be "driven" behavior, i.e., the energy level of the child will seem to be inappropriate or dispropor-

[41] E. M. Bower, P. J. Tashnovian, and C. A. Larson, *A Process for Early Identification of Emotionally Disturbed Children* (Sacramento, California State Department of Education, 1959).

tionate to the task. The child may play with an intensity and frenzy which bodes ill to anyone or anything interfering. He may be unable to obey rules in school even after repeated and varied contacts with accepting or disciplining adults. Other children are able to change and adapt based upon their analysis of the reward and punishment system. The emotional child has relatively little freedom to adapt. He is often regarded as especially stubborn and recalcitrant since the usual influence techniques of reward, punishment, recognition, praise, and the like are relatively ineffective in influencing his behavior. Or he may be regarded as a "real pushover," i.e., influenced almost completely by the wishes and ideas of others. . . . In healthy emotional development the individual has sufficient ego strength to vary his personality approximately in accordance with the situation and at the same time to maintain a sufficient core of self in all situations. For example, one is not expected to be the same at church as at a party, yet the differences cannot be so radical as to involve complete changes in personality.

[The child's] ideas about the teacher or his peers may be somewhat distorted. For example, he may see the teacher as a punishing, threatening adult and classmates as competitive siblings constantly outdoing him in reading, drawing, or sports.

The Continuum of Degree: Behavior related to emotional problems may be displayed in transient, temporary, pervasive, or intense types of behavior. To complete our definition, it would be necessary to establish a continuum upon which the degree of handicap can be perceived and perhaps estimated, especially as it relates to possible action by the school. One could begin such a continuum with (a) children who experience and demonstrate the normal problems of everyday living, growing, exploration and reality testing. There are some, however, who can be observed as (b) children who develop a greater number and degree of symptoms of emotional problems as a result of a crisis or traumatic experience. Such a crisis or traumatic experience may be death of father, birth of sibling, divorce of parents, brain or body injury, school entrance, junior high school entrance, adolescence, etc. Some move beyond this point and may be described as (c) children in whom symptoms persist to some extent beyond normal expectations but who can manage an adequate school adjustment. The next group would include (d) children with fixed and recurring symptoms of emotional disturbance who can, with help, maintain some positive relationships in a school setting. Beyond this are (e) children with fixed and recurring symptoms of emotional difficulties who are best educated in a residential school setting or temporarily in a home setting. Past studies[42] and present research[43] indicate that the last three groups include about 10 per cent of the school population.

> The classroom teacher can do little to improve the home situation for the child. If he becomes aware of of a problem at home, a request for outside help by a social worker or clinic should be made. He can, however, provide the child with a secure situation in the classroom. The teacher who is aware of the fact that a child has a serious problem at home and yet makes rigid, unyielding demands of him in the classroom performs a disservice to the child and the teaching profession.

> In some instances, when the teacher learns of clothing or food needs or that a child needs a place to study, he may be able to take more direct action. In most situations, however, an accepting, warm, rewarding, concerned teacher can be of considerable psychological support and may have a major influence on the child's life.

> SOME ASPECTS OF THE FAILURE SYNDROME: All too frequently schools create a failure syndrome because a

---

[42] Mike Gorman, *Every Other Bed* (New York, World Publishing Co., 1956) , p. 23.
[43] Bower, Tashnovian and Larson, *op. cit.*, pp. 57–58.

child's problem goes unnoticed or untreated for a long time. Other teachers do not appear to accept the fact that when there is failure, there must be a cause. Thus, when a child fails, the teacher must attempt to determine the cause as soon as possible, so that help may be given. Too often, children are asked to perform complicated tasks even when they have failed to learn the necessary previous skills. In later grades these children can become the more serious behavior problems.

Society and the schools, which reflect society's attitudes, contradict themselves in the way they act toward the child who is failing. It is generally accepted that failure behavior should occur in the safety of the school setting, where the child can be helped by an understanding teacher. However, the contrary is accepted practice. *If a child fails in school, he is usually punished.* He then learns to make sure he is correct before he tries new behavior, thereby reducing creativity, or he ceases to try at all.

In an article entitled "The Decision to Fail," Bruno Bettleheim[44] finds that when a child is rejected or unable to be the best,

He may then arrive at the conviction that he can gain status only by being the worst. In this way he attracts attention to himself; true, in a negative way, but attention nevertheless.

The learner who does poorly, on the other hand, is convinced he can never make the grade. He is impelled to stop learning by his wish to maintain self-respect. Believing that he will fail even if he makes his best efforts, he protects himself by deciding not to learn. Then he will be able to tell himself that his failure is not due to inability, but to a deliberate act of will. Hence it is not rare for such a child to feel he can gain more

44 Bruno Bettleheim, "The Decision to Fail," *The School Review*, Vol. 69, Winter 1961, pp. 391–392.

status or self-respect through not learning than through diligent application.

In other instances, when a child begins to fail, the teacher may simply feel that if he really applied himself or if he would practice more, he would be able to pass. The teacher's action is then either to put tremendous pressure on the child with such devices as threatening him, calling in his parents, or sending him to the principal, or to give him considerable additional material of the same kind to do after school and at home. The child who is unable to cope with the work, regardless of the pressure or the additional work, is confused, becomes anxious, withdrawn or hostile to the teacher and the school, or he may have a serious breakdown.

Finally, some teachers simply tell the child he is a failure. They believe that the child is incapable of doing the work, and they pity him and tell him that he really is a poor student. Then they feel free to ignore him, fail him or give him different or separate work which he may or may not be able to do. The child sees himself as a failure and frequently quits trying.

IV. School and Community Variables

This category catches many elements in the school or community which can cause problems or situations that interfere with learning. In determining the cause of a problem, evaluation of these areas should not be neglected.

A. Many school systems have insufficient funds to employ the necessary professional pupil personnel services staff. If the community has no agencies which provide speech, social work, health and psychological assistance, the child having a problem which is too complex to be handled by the teacher receives no help and can become more seriously involved. All too often, even where services do exist, they are minimal, requiring long waiting periods. Many are poorly organized, with little communication among the various disciplines. The school is frequently an island with little liaison with community agencies.

B. Theoretically, teachers and school administrators never complete their training. They need to continue to learn so that they can improve. In almost all school systems the amount of time that is devoted to the supervision of a teacher is less than a clerk would have in industry. Many factors account for this negative situation. These include: lack of public support for supervision, the concept that a teacher is a finished product when he comes out of college, the relative lack of sound supervisory training, teachers' misunderstanding of what supervision is and the growth of the notion that the classroom belongs to the teacher. These factors frequently lead to the stagnation of the teacher's approach to children, thus causing them further problems.

C. In order to provide the maximum conditions for learning, each child needs the best environment possible. Many school buildings are fifty and sixty years old, unable to accommodate new programs and practices. Many are depressing, have poor furniture and are overcrowded. Under these conditions children do not learn as well as they could, and all too frequently in these situations learning problems are created or exaggerated.

A child needs a place at home to work and study. If he lives in crowded quarters, if there is little or no equipment to stimulate him, his motivation for learning is diminished. It is difficult to concentrate on learning if there is constant hunger. Some children live in homes which have no routines. Eating and sleeping occur rather haphazardly. Under these conditions, a child is in a constantly disorganized state and he frequently cannot cope with the demands of the school.

A community shows its support for the educational enterprise by providing supportive activities, either on its own or in cooperation with other communities. Lack of adequate library facilities, museums, cultural activities, etc., sometimes hinders the growth of the children in a community.

D. Many schools still maintain, in the face of a changing student body, essentially the same programs they had fifty years ago. A careful assessment of the needs of each child would go a long way toward assisting the school in its effort to meet these needs and providing the programs which would assure the successful attainment of the school goals. It is obvious that all children cannot achieve at the same level each year. The fact that students fail and then leave school is sufficient evidence for the need to change.

E. Previous discussions have alluded to the difficulties of children that are caused by problems in the home. Suffice it to say that a careful evaluation of the home may be important in determining the reason for a child's failure in school.

A School Program for Children Who Have Problems That Interfere with Learning

Since each child is unique in the way he learns and varies from others in his achievement, the schools must always strive to meet individual needs. In planning a school program for children who have problems that interfere with their achieving the goals we have helped set for them, several principles must be considered:

1. The child must be maintained in as close to normal a situation as possible. He should be kept living at home, attending a regular class, in a school with children from his neighborhood if at all possible.
2. If special help and/or placement is necessary, this must always be regarded as temporary or transitional and the the child returned to a normal situation as soon as possible.
3. Labels or classifications are not enough for the teacher. They are frequently irrelevant or harmful. He needs specific, detailed help in each area of program development for each child who has a problem which is too severe for him to handle alone.

Reynolds[45] offers a conceptual framework for dealing with children with learning problems and a hierarchy of services which emphasize that:

1. Most children can be handled in the regular classroom by giving some assistance either to the teacher or to the child and by reducing the number of children in the class.
2. Children are moved up through the hierarchy of programs only as far as necessary, and they are moved down as soon as it is possible. It has been found that the farther removed they are from the regular classes, the less accepted they are by their peers, other parents, teachers, and the general public; the more expensive the program, the more specialized the staff must be, and the more involved other agencies become.

The bottom level in the chart (Figure VI) represents the

FIGURE VI

PROGRAMS FOR CHILDREN WITH
LEARNING PROBLEMS[46]

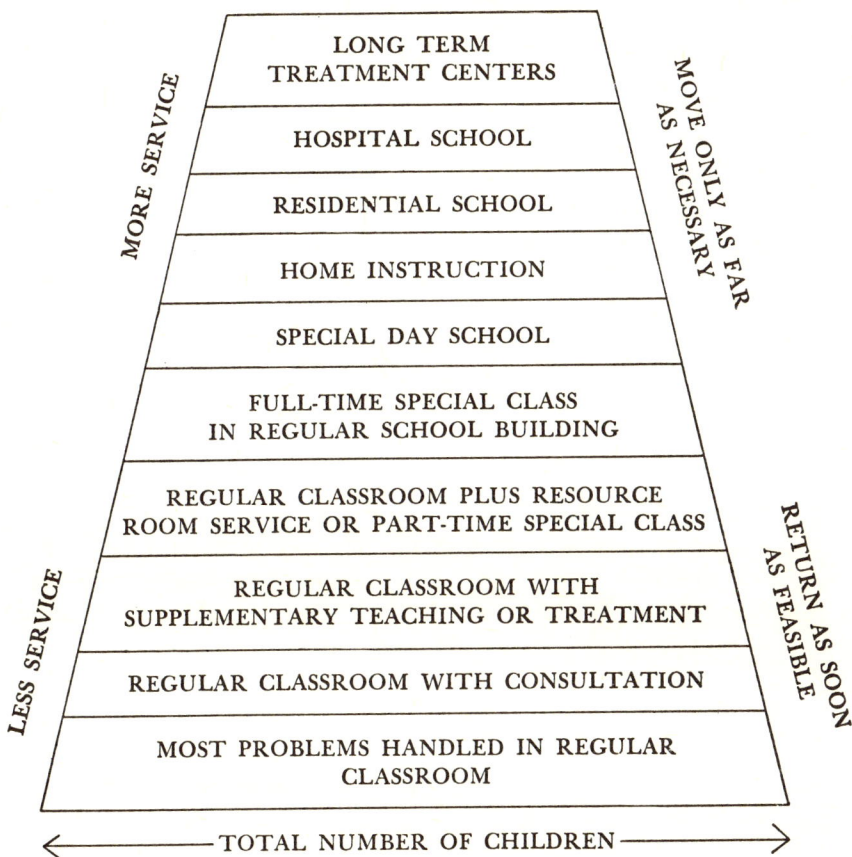

LONG TERM
TREATMENT CENTERS

HOSPITAL SCHOOL

RESIDENTIAL SCHOOL

HOME INSTRUCTION

SPECIAL DAY SCHOOL

FULL-TIME SPECIAL CLASS
IN REGULAR SCHOOL BUILDING

REGULAR CLASSROOM PLUS RESOURCE
ROOM SERVICE OR PART-TIME SPECIAL CLASS

REGULAR CLASSROOM WITH
SUPPLEMENTARY TEACHING OR TREATMENT

REGULAR CLASSROOM WITH CONSULTATION

MOST PROBLEMS HANDLED IN REGULAR
CLASSROOM

MORE SERVICE

LESS SERVICE

MOVE ONLY AS FAR AS NECESSARY

RETURN AS SOON AS FEASIBLE

← TOTAL NUMBER OF CHILDREN →

[46] Adapted from Reynolds, *op. cit.*

largest number of children with learning problems, those who can be taught by the regular class teacher who has received some additional training. The next level, referred to as "regular classroom with consultation," includes children with whom the teacher can deal when special service personnel are available for consultation.

The third level is for children with more complex problems, who need specialized teaching or treatments. They may need such specialists as speech correctionists and remedial reading teachers. Disturbed children who need brief periods of counseling are also included in this level.

Children who need an extended period of help should utilize a resource room or be included part-time in a special class. These may be children with more serious visual handicaps, emotional problems, or other learning difficulties. These children should be given home instruction or be included in a full-time special class program, special day school, residential school, hospital school, or long-term treatment center *only when they cannot profit from the regular classroom.* They would remain in such programs only for as long as necessary and move as rapidly as possible back toward a more normal situation. Referral to programs in the upper levels of this chart might be based on such factors as delinquency and poor home environment. Referrals would also be made in extremely rare situations when the problem is so serious and complicated that very specialized care and treatment are needed for an extended period of time.

The concept of a dynamic, flexible program is evident in the notion of the flow of youngsters from one type of program to another, based on their changing needs. It is necessary if we are to achieve the goal of individual planning for each child with a learning problem and maximizing his education. Schools can be helped to plan programs for the vast majority of their children by utilizing the approach presented in this hierarchy of services.

CHAPTER 6

Suggested Activities and Practices for Overcoming Learning Problems

Choosing Appropriate Activities

Every teacher of children with learning difficulties should try using the problem-solving or diagnostic method outlined in the introduction. (Figure I, from the introduction, is repeated here for the reader's convenience.) In the process, when he has exhausted all the activities he knows to help overcome a child's problems, he may want to look at those listed below. The activities are organized by groups according to the outline below.

Outline of Activities and Practices

I. Activities and Practices Adaptable to a Wide Variety of Uses
   A. Games and other activities

II. Activities to Improve General Developmental Skills

   A. Auditory perception
   B. Body image
   C. Concept formation
   D. Concentration

Figure I

A PROBLEM-SOLVING TEACHING APPROACH FOR CHILDREN WHO HAVE LEARNING DIFFICULTIES

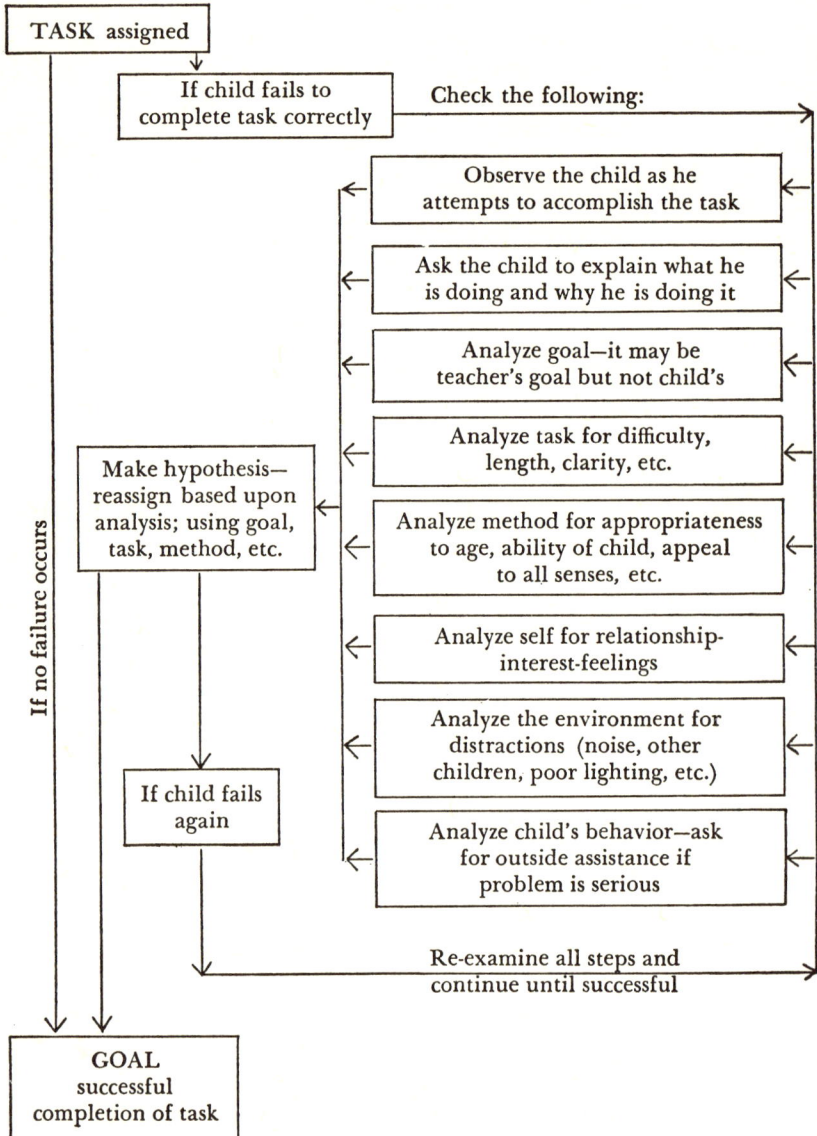

  E. Fine motor
  F. Gross motor
  G. Kinesthetic
  H. Laterality, directionality
   I. Listening
  J. Memory, auditory
  K. Memory, visual
  L. Sensory, motor
  M. Tactile
  N. Vision perception
  O. Vocabulary building, language development

III. Activities for Improving Reading Skills

  A. Work attack
  B. Motivation
  C. Fluency
  D. Comprehension
  E. Practice
  F. Accuracy

IV. Activities for Improving Skills in Mathematics

  A. Numeration
  B. Non-numerical concepts
  C. Place value
  D. Processes or combinations of processes
  E. Fractions
  F. Money
  G. Time
  H. Systems of measurement

 V. Activities for Improving Behavior Skills

  A. Creating a healthy environment
  B. Feelings about self
  C. Relationships with others
  D. Individual relationships to environment

The teacher should attempt to determine which problem prevents the child from improving his comprehension, and to form a hypothesis as to how to overcome it. He may choose a change in the method or give attention to motivation, a new task, a private conference, some assessment, etc., as most appropriate. If it is a new activity that is needed, he should choose one which is directly related to overcoming the problem.

Principles for Use of Activities

Certain general rules concerning these activities should be clearly understood before they are used.

1. There are no magic solutions to children's specific difficulties. Helping them requires a painstaking and creative effort. The teacher may fail several times before he succeeds.
2. Since children enjoy games if they are presented without pressure, they are more likely to learn through them than through more formal lessons.
3. Activities should be selected on the basis of the teacher's feeling that they will help overcome a specific problem, and should not be used as busywork. The teacher must be able to give a clear explanation as to why he chose an activity, both to himself and to others who ask.
4. The whole approach of this book requires that the teacher use a creative-adaptive approach to the problems children present. Therefore, these activities are to be changed and adapted to fit the needs of a particular child and the individual talents of each teacher. There is no requirement for the use of the activities as they appear in the book. If there is any mandate, it is that they should be adapted to fit each new situation.
5. Children should be given a choice of the activities they

would like and enjoy and those they feel may help them.

6. Activities listed under one category are also appropriate for other problems.

7. The activities and games are not meant to be used to develop fierce competition. In any race there is only one winner and many losers. Let the child compete against his own previous performance, not the performances of others.

8. If an activity is not successful in accomplishing the teacher's purpose, he should give it up and choose another. Most children who have problems in learning do not need additional failures. The emphasis is on successful experiences.

9. Do not substitute these activities for any that the child really enjoys.

10. Even if some activities work, do not continue to use them over and over again. Vary the activities. Novelty increases motivation.

11. A most relevant factor to a child's success is the teacher's attitude. *An optimistic, encouraging teacher can often achieve near miracles.* A pessimistic, negative teacher can destroy a child's desire to learn.

Obviously, the activities listed in this chapter are only *samples* of the type that can be found. The teacher will add to these as he scans new books and magazines. One activity suggests another. Some activities are just for fun. Don't overlook these.

I. Activities and Practices Adaptable to a Wide Variety of Uses

Certain activities and practices have general use in helping overcome problems that interfere with learning. They can be adapted to a wide variety of areas limited only by the imagination of the teachers.

GAMES CAN MAKE LEARNING FUN. Although games sometimes take on a serious note and may even be quite brutal, (e.g., football and boxing), most people consider them fun. If they are not misused or overused, games can provide the teacher with an excellent device for making learning fun. There is no law which says that learning must be painful. The following suggestions should be considered in planning games to help ensure that the children continue to enjoy them:

1. See that the losers remain part of the game.
2. In selecting appropriate games, consider the group interest, age, ability, attire, play area, equipment, and objectives.
3. Have the children choose, plan and control the games.
4. Be flexible. If one game does not seem to be going well, change to another. Do not be afraid to change the rules if it looks as though a change will make the game more fun—but check with the children first.
5. Stop the game while the children are still enjoying it and asking for more.

A BRIEF NOTE ON "LOSERS." Games should be fun for all the children. It seems ridiculous then to make games as punishing as some other aspects of the school program. Eliminating children from the game when they fail to give the response or performance called for can be disastrous to them. It should be the aim of the teacher to keep all the children participating at all times. Having point scores, rotating the child who is the leader, giving additional help to the person who misses are examples of how to keep the games fun for all the children.

A. GAMES AND ACTIVITIES ADAPTABLE TO A WIDE VARIETY OF USES

　　1. Bingo: Bingo has many variations. It can be organized to provide practice with new words,

opposite words, punctuation, synonyms, numbers, addition, subtraction, multiplication, division, fractions and many others. A supply of paper with squares may be duplicated and the teacher or the children may enter in the items to be used.

2. Magic tricks: The teacher with a bag full of tricks can often motivate the child who cannot be motivated any other way. Many tricks are mechanical and may be purchased through the mail or in a big city magic shop. Telling a particular child how the trick is done may help you reach him.

3. Scrapbooks: Children love to cut and paste and make scrapbooks. A little care in creating a nice cover and any topic can lend itself to "My _____ Book." It may be pictures for safety, space flight, stories, colors, cars, etc.

4. Tape recorder: Once it becomes a part of his repertoire the tape recorder is a tool whose use is limited only by the imagination of the teacher. It can be used to motivate, initiate activities, bring in information, tape record activities, play back information or events, reteach, dramatize, send taped lessons home, correct speech, develop language, make reports, etc.

5. Treasure hunts: A great deal of learning can be part of finding treasures. The activities that can be included are: making the treasure, hiding the treasure, making a map, making up clues that lead to the treasure (riddles, rhymes, etc.), teamwork, interpreting oral, written and visual clues, following a treasure map, telling time, etc. Treasure hunts can be held indoors or out.

6. Typewriter: This instrument can sometimes help a teacher when he has been unable to motivate a child or when a child has a serious writing prob-

lem. Although costly when compared to pencil and paper, it nevertheless represents a skill all the children in the class may eventually have to learn. It is sometimes suggested that all children should be typing by the sixth grade.

7. Putting on a show: Probably no activity is harder on the children and the teacher but more satisfying than putting on some type of show. There are all types. These include puppet, marionette, magic, talent, drama, songs, etc. Shows may be used to entertain your own class, the class next door, your entire grade, the whole school, PTA's, old people's institutions, nursery school children, etc. Some teachers feel that they have no time to have the children plan and execute a show since the children must complete all the work prescribed in the curriculum guide. Although there is little research on this subject, many teachers are certain that children learn to read, write, compute, improve their feeling about themselves and ability to work with other children far more through a show or performance than they do in everyday lessons. For some children, planning and putting on a show is an excellent technique for helping them overcome their learning problems.

8. Role playing and dramatization: Role playing is an important technique for the teacher to know and to use. It can be used with groups of children at any age to teach problem-solving, help a student understand himself, deal with a wide variety of classroom problems, improve the classroom learning climate, and improve interpersonal relations. Teachers who can use this activity find its use is limited only by their imagination. This technique has been rather thoroughly researched by Ronald

Lippit.[47] The results of many years of study have proved the considerable values and validity of this approach.

The teacher must take time to prepare for the use of role playing. To gain understanding and assurance, the teacher should practice this technique in small groups with single situations. The sequence of steps in role playing as suggested by Chesler and Fox[48] are:

1. Preparation and instruction. This first part of the activity includes "problem solution, warm up, and general and specific instructions to participants and audience.[49]

2. Dramatic action. Students should be given sufficient time to be able to feel the part and immerse themselves in the character.

3. Debriefing. Immediately after the action the children should be asked to assume their normal roles.

4. Discussion. Then the audience and the players should discuss the roles that were played.

5. Evaluation. In order to make full use of these techniques, it is essential that the students help the teacher to evaluate the activity and suggest what they learned, what they might want to do in the future, and how it might be improved.

B. EXPERIENCE CHARTS AND CHILDREN'S OWN STORYBOOKS: Children are generally motivated to learn more about things that they have done themselves. The teacher of younger children should have the

[47] Ronald Lippit, "Understanding Classroom Social Relations and Learning," Chicago Science Research Associates, 1966.

[48] Mark Chesler and Robert Fox, "Role Playing Methods in the Classroom," Chicago Science Research Associates, 1966.

[49] *Ibid.*, p. 22.

students dictate the stories as he writes them on large paper so he can save them. The children may copy their stories. As children are more able, they may write of their own experiences and make up their own readers. Children's stories sometimes reveal something about how they think, their problems and what they enjoy.

C. Word Games: This type of game develops many areas. Children can be helped to improve their language skills, concepts, auditory discrimination, etc. The teacher can invent many forms. Some of the more common are, "Say the opposite," "Name another word that means the same," "What words sound like _____" (homonyms), "Can you say a rhyme?", "Name the family this word is in," etc.

D. Special Award Box: Have a drawer in your desk with cards in it. On each card place a picture (for younger children) or a word or phrase for the more able. When a child does something you feel should be rewarded, let him take a card out of the box. If he can tell you what it is he is rewarded. The reward can be lollypops, candy, pencils, erasers, colored paper, small books, etc.

II. Activities to Improve General Developmental Skills

A. Auditory Perception

1. Have the child close his eyes and try to identify different sounds (e.g., tearing of paper, a high note, a low note, a pencil being sharpened, running water). If necessary, first show the child the objects you are using so he can identify the sound with the object.

2. "What do you hear?" Choose a time of the day when pupils can hear sounds in the street, halls

or surroundings. Have them identify as many as they can.

3. Blindfold a child. Ring a bell in various parts of the room. He must point to the spot that the sound comes from.

4. Bell the cat. Blindfolded children try to catch the "cat" as he runs around the room wearing a bell or making a noise.

5. Near or far. Children listen to determine how far away the sound is; do the same with loud or soft sounds; have them group sounds to be certain the concepts about sound are learned. (Loud, soft, bells, drums, etc.)

6. Have children experience the sounds of different musical instruments; then play simple instrumental records and have them pick out the different instruments heard.

7. Find words which rhyme. Read aloud jingles in which the rhyme is quite apparent. Call attention to the rhyming words and encourage children to find them and suggest other words that rhyme with them. Tape recordings or records may be used.

8. Give children rhyme riddles (e.g., name three keys that are too big to put in your pocket: donkey, monkey, turkey) ; (name two toes that are not on your feet: potatoes, tomatoes, etc.) .

9. Riddle rhymes. Encourage the children to make up rhymes containing riddles. When they get into the swing of it, they really enjoy this (e.g., I rhyme with "boy"; you play with me; what am I?) .

10. Have child listen for and identify a preselected melody of music threaded through other music.

11. Have child spell words aloud to learn them.

12. Blindfold a child. Have another call his name. He must identify the caller.
13. Tapping game. Teacher taps loud, soft, etc.; children are asked to reproduce taps.

B. BODY IMAGE

1. Have child assume different body positions while standing in front of a mirror (e.g., jump, clap hands, arms out, arms up, hands on head, etc.). If he can, have him tell or describe what he is doing.
2. Play "Simon Says" in front of a mirror. Have child observe and name his actions.
3. Make large cardboard cutouts of pieces of the entire body. Let child assemble pieces in the correct positions. Do the same thing with parts of the face, use clothes etc.
4. Draw partially completed figures or faces on chalkboard or on paper. Let child complete them.
5. Draw figures of body on the board, part by part, child touches the same part of himself as it is drawn.

C. CONCEPT FORMATION

1. Give child large assortment of objects. Ask him to sort things in order according to size—from the biggest to the smallest.
2. Have child compare groups of objects which are grossly different in number and tell you which is more or less. Use anything available around the schoolroom. Gradually have child estimate quantities more nearly equal size. Use concrete objects first, having child handle objects. Then move to pictures of things.

3. Have child do exercises involving objects: jump over a block, crawl under a table, go around a desk, stand in a box, step out of a circle. Use a game form (e.g., obstacle race). Child should say or shout what he is doing as he does it. First he can play a follow-the-leader type of game; then he does as you "say."

4. Ask child to pile *lots* of blocks in a truck. Use terms "many," "more than one," "one," "all alone."

5. Have a child place objects in boxes or cups arranged in line. Egg cartons, muffin tins, may be used. Teacher and child verbalize "enough," "too many," "need some more."

6. What do you do with it? Paste pictures on cards or have child look through a magazine. Have him tell what one does with objects (e.g., bed—sleep; dress—wear it, etc.).

7. Have children make up scrapbooks of fruit, houses, people, etc., to learn concept of families, related ideas, things and words.

8. Act out pictures and organize them in categories (e.g. bathroom, kitchen, car articles). Have children tell about them. (Later have children organize them.)

D. CONCENTRATION: (Except for the possible need for medical care in order to help the child control his behavior, the problem of concentration is treated with the same techniques as if brain injury were not a factor.)

1. Reward the completion of *each* activity in a meaningful way (e.g., juice and crackers, games, rest, painting). What is meaningful to one child is not to another.

2. Direct the child's attention to some action you are taking which is of interest to him. Try to get him to focus on what you are doing for a short period of time. Gradually increase the time. You may tell a short story, perform a magic trick, etc.

3. Give the child only one task at a time. Keep everything else off his desk.

4. Provide an area in the room which is relatively isolated (use a screen when appropriate). Call it a private office. Have children go to it when they are being distracted. It must be seen as a way to help the child to work out problems and must not be used as punishment.

5. Make certain the task is of interest to the child. Ask him to complete a task of short duration.

6. Shorten the amount of work, and therefore the time it takes to do it. Relate work to the level of child's ability to concentrate, gradually increasing the amount. Change activities frequently.

E. FINE MOTOR

1. Cutting with scissors is an excellent exercise for fine motor practice. The first task should be just cutting through a piece of paper; gradually move child toward more complicated tasks, shapes, figures, etc.

2. Play games involving fine motor activities (e.g., ball and jacks, relay races involving carrying a potato or a spoon, rhythm instruments, drawing pictures, etc.)

3. Help child make pot holders on a weaving loom.

4. Use sewing cards, which are large and easy for the child to handle. This may take a good deal of concentration for some child—for a time, teacher may need to work individually with child.

5. Have child trace, color and perform everyday activities (e.g., buttoning, lacing, tying, open and close zippers, use staplers and other simple tools to develop motor control). Set up a sequence if necessary.
6. Have child prepare refreshments: make cocoa, Kool-ade; spread jelly, peanut butter, butter, honey; pour milk from a bottle or a pitcher, etc.

F. Gross Motor

1. Have child do exercises involving objects (e.g., jump over a block, crawl under a table, go around a desk, stand in a box, step out of a circle) Try an obstacle race or a follow-the-leader type of game.
2. Draw boxes on floor or ground. Then have child step in certain numbered boxes.
3. Have child walk along a wide board (2 x 6) placed on two low blocks. At first, hold the child's hand until he develops some confidence. Have him walk backwards (e.g., with eyes opened, eyes closed).
4. Have child practice on a balancing board (a board about two feet long placed on a horizontal cylinder). The child places his feet near each end of the board and tries to maintain his balance.
5. Have child do rhythms and dances (e.g., move to the right, stamp your feet, slap your sides, etc.).
6. Find poems and songs that call for movements (look in primary school books). Play and sing with children.
7. Involve child in games that stress action (e.g., "Simon Says": Raise your right hand, Loopy Loo; put your right foot in, etc.).

8. Have child play imaginative games: pulling horse and cart—really use muscles to push or pull load; pushing backwards or sideways; storm game—run around, arms outstretched (wind); tiptoe (rain); jump up and down (hard rain), etc.

9. Have child become involved in running, skipping, galloping, hopping, walking sideways, backward, etc.

G. KINESTHETIC (motion or muscle movement)

1. Have child draw picture of object and word in the air.

2. To help a child improve his writing, have him close his eyes and write on the chalkboard.

3. Have the child count as he walks. Negative numbers may be learned by walking backwards.

4. Have the child clap as he counts so he gets feeling of number differences.

5. Have child do the action as he says or reads a word or follows a verbal or written instruction.

H. LATERALITY, DIRECTIONALITY

1. Have child make colored bracelets to wear on right hand (red) and left hand (green). He then wears these when direction activities are going on (e.g., "Wonder Ball"—children are seated in circle and follow commands, "Pass the ball right," "now to the left," etc. When music stops, child who has ball is eliminated. Change direction frequently.)

2. Ask each child in turn to stand, to raise his right hand, put it down, then raise his left hand and put it down. Make sure each child has a red and blue crayon. Then play a simple game of following directions such as, Place your *right* hand *over* your desk. Put your *left* hand *on* your head. Put your red crayon on the *left* side of your desk. Put your

blue crayon on the *right*. Put your crayon box *under* your desk."

3. A group with less skill may need practice in a game of "Follow the Leader" in which the teacher, standing with her back to the group, carries out the actions as she gives the directions for a showing of right and left hands.

4. Give each child two pieces of paper; tell him to trace around the fingers and thumb of his left hand first; on the other paper do the same with his right hand. Place the drawing of the left hand in the upper left-hand corner of his desk and the right hand in the upper right-hand corner. Then say, "These will help you to remember which is left and which is right."

5. Using a printed card, cover words to be read with a zipper. Open the zipper from left to right, each time exposing the words to be read.

6. Have child put pictures in sequential order according to numbers at the bottom. Assemble according to number and then lay them down from left to right. Increase the number of pictures as child improves.

7. Play games, songs and dances which call for movement of right and left parts of the body (e.g., Simon Says; Loopy Loo, etc.) .

8. Set up a hop-scotch game on the floor. When child hops, make sure he does it with his right foot (hops on right side) , then with his left foot on left side.

I. LISTENING (see activities in section A, auditory perception)

1. What word is missing? Explain that you are going to tell or read a story and that you will pause at

certain places and leave out a word. The child is to supply the missing words. It may sometimes be necessary for the teacher to complete the phrase or sentence in which the missing word appears. As the words are given, write them on the blackboard.

2. Wait for a quiet time. Have children listen for sounds they can hear.

3. Ask children to write or draw a picture of sounds they hear during the day. Later change to unusual sounds. Give those who hear usual sounds well an assignment which requires greater discrimination.

J. MEMORY, AUDITORY

(Activities which use other senses may be helpful in improving auditory memory.)

1. Tap or beat out number combinations and sequence. Child taps out the answer or sequence.

2. Involve child in singing simple songs. Then have child sing from memory.

3. Read a simple story. Ask child to draw three or more picture sequences, like a cartoon strip, while you read the story. Ask the child to retell the story from the cartoons.

4. Have child listen to recordings of rhymes in order to learn to identify and remember sounds.

5. Play a game. One child says something and a second child tries to repeat it. If correct, he takes the lead. As child's ability to remember increases, increase the number of children involved in the game and its complexity.

6. The suitcase game. Child says, "I am going on a trip and in my suitcase I will pack a _____."
Here the child names some article like a comb. In order to add another article, next child must

repeat the original saying plus all other articles named.

7. Send child on errands with short oral messages to relate.

8. Play "Simon Says." Give two and then more commands at one time.

9. After giving directions for games and activities, allow the children to take turns in giving directions for those each would like to do.

10. Find something the child wants to do that needs direction. Give him short oral directions to be followed. Gradually increase the length of the directions, thus causing the child to pay closer attention and to concentrate.

11. Play "Giant Steps," in which the child must remember to say "May I?" before doing what is commanded of him, or play "Simon Says," in which the child must again listen for a specific phrase before following through an action.

12. Teach short poems or songs by rote. This will develop child's confidence and his ability to concentrate. These should be short and enjoyable to the child.

13. Have the child act out a story which has been read to the class. This child should be given the easiest and shortest part to act out. This can gradually be increased.

K. MEMORY, VISUAL

1. What do you do with it? Paste pictures of objects on cards or simply look through magazines. Have child tell what he does with objects (e.g., bed—sleep in it; dress—wear it, etc.) .

2. Write a question on the board. Use pictures for

unknown words. Erase it. Have child answer the question by discussion, writing or drawing.

3. A touch game. First player touches and names an object. Second player touches and names the same object and adds another one by touching and naming it.

4. Using a slide projector, teacher flashes a picture or words on the screen. Then child tells what he saw.

5. Show a short film story without sound. Ask child to tell story or reproduce it in pictures.

6. Ask child to make a visit or plan a trip, then to describe what he has seen.

7. Have a child look carefully at a picture with a number of things in it. Remove the picture and ask for a list of things in the picture.

8. Place several objects on a table. Have child turn away while an object is removed. When he turns back, he tries to identify which object has been removed.

9. Set up a craft lesson which has pictured instructions. Let child study directions and then proceed with making object. Start with two- or three-step projects.

10. Make a set of a dozen circles, squares, etc. Cut them in two, varying the cuts so that no two are alike. Give one half to one child, one half to another. Let children find those that match. Give points to winners.

11. Have the child tell or write or draw pictures of what he saw on his way to school. Child might add to list each day.

12. Place two or more checkers on a checkerboard. Have child view placement briefly, then place his own checkers in same spots on his own board

without looking at the model. Increase complexity.

13. Tell children to look in windows of neighborhood stores, or at bulletin boards in school, etc. Each day teacher chooses a location and asks children if they can remember what they saw. Have them go to look.

14. Draw a picture but leave out a part. Have child draw in missing part.

15. Have the child draw picture of a room as he remembers it. Then compare the picture to the actual room.

L. SENSORY, MOTOR (Eye-hand, Auditory-Speech, Eye-Speech, Auditory-Hand)

1. "Do it if you can." Make a set of cards each having a particular direction on it. Have child act out direction (e.g., run to the table). If direction is carried out correctly, child keeps card.

2. "Can you do it?" Make a set of cards each having a picture of someone doing something a child can do. Child selects a card and performs the act. After he performs the action, he can tell you what he saw and what he did. At first, try to keep child from verbalizing while he performs act.

3. Have child trace previously drawn letters, figures, numbers.

4. Have child draw letters, figures and numbers outlined by dots.

5. Purchase or make a board with openings for forms and animals. Have child place correct pieces in correct openings.

6. Cutting with scissors is an excellent exercise for eye-hand coordination practice. The first task should be just cutting through a piece of paper,

gradually moving toward more complicated tasks, shapes, figures, etc.

7. "What do you do with it?" Paste pictures on cards or simply look through magazines. Have child tell what one does with objects (e.g., bed—sleep in it; dress—wear it, etc.).

8. Have the child join dots to form patterns. Start with simple activity, increase complexity.

9. Have the child carry out simple requests such as, "Please close the door," etc.

10. Have the child choose a game to be played by the class and have him give oral directions for the game.

11. Play games which involve throwing, catching, etc.

12. Have child connect dotted lines, making a picture. Let him place a carbon paper and another sheet behind the paper with the dots to see how the picture comes out.

13. Have a child construct something, then have him make up oral or written directions for another child to follow (on his own or as teams).

14. Set up a sequence of directions from simple to rather complicated. Devise various ways of giving directions (e.g., tape recording, picture form, stick figures, cartoons, blackboard, written, etc.).

M. TACTILE PERCEPTION (feel or touch)

1. Use sandpaper, felt or heavy cardboard for letters and numbers. Have child trace or feel with fingers as he says what they are.

2. "What is it?" Put familiar objects into a bag. Have child reach in and feel the object and then name it. If named correctly, it is held by child. Have child verbalize what he feels and how he came to his conclusion.

3. Pictures that a child can feel can be made as collages. Odds and ends of paper, cloth, leaves, cotton, pipecleaners, doilies may be pasted on tagboard or wrapping paper.

4. Have children paste pipecleaners on predrawn design or words. Let them feel it after it is completed.

5. Write a word on the blackboard. Let the child erase it as he traces it with his finger.

6. Write word on flat clay surface so that word is indented. Have child trace the word with his finger. Wet beach sand may be substituted and may work better for some children.

7. Use hard pencil and write so that cardboard surface becomes indented. Have children trace with finger. Another way is to punch holes in the cardboard.

N. VISION PERCEPTION

1. Have the child trace various shaped blocks as they are handed to him.

2. Have child match picture and concrete object.

3. Child reproduces peg patterns made by teacher (or by child).

4. Have child place cardboard cutouts over corresponding objects, shapes and sizes.

5. "What do you do with it?" Paste pictures on cards or have child look through magazines. Have him tell what one does with various objects (e.g., bed—sleep in it; dress—wear it).

6. Attach a ribbon to hula hoop and have child keep his eyes on the ribbon as hoop turns.

7. Have child follow movements you make on chalkboard. Make circles, ellipses and spirals. He should move his eyes without moving his head.

8. Attach an object such as a football to a string. Tape letters on. Attach overhead and let swing like a pendulum. Child must identify the letters.

9. Have child separate small objects, such as varied colored beads, into piles according to *color*.

10. Have a bag full of the same, similar and different objects of various sizes. Have children sort these according to size.

11. Draw pictures of forms and shapes on blackboard. Have child touch those that have the same shape.

12. Have a bag of different-shaped objects—round, square, triangular. Have child sort according to shape.

13. Have children bring in pictures of themselves. Hang them on the wall. Print name under each one. Have one child match another child with picture, find his own, etc.

14. Child stands in front of mirror and holds up objects, then names them as he sees them.

15. Write numbers from 1 to 15 in consecutive order on the board in three columns about 12 inches apart. Have the child stand six feet from board and look at the numbers. Have child call out each number in time with signal and point toward each number selected.

16. Play dominoes using cards with pictures or symbols on each side instead of numbers. Make up cards using duplicate pictures and follow domino game sequence.

17. Have child tell you the names for all the things he can see.

18. Find familiar pictures. Cut out a piece. Have child identify missing piece.

O. VOCABULARY BUILDING, LANGUAGE DEVELOPMENT

1. After the child has listened to a story or read one silently, have him list certain *action* words that help tell the story (e.g., "rumbling," "running," "barking," "waving," etc.). Call attention to the fact that each word tells about something that happened.

2. Telephone. Get a set of telephones. Have child choose a topic to talk about and have the child call and talk to other children. Teacher can talk to students, using phone. Leave phones for independent activities.

3. Play a game of opposites. Say a word. The child who says the opposite first gets the word card. Play with small group.

4. Play a game. Have child write his own stories. Mimeograph them so that each child has a copy. Have the child go through the story and substitute synonyms for as many words as possible. Let child read his stories.

5. Change the order in which pictures or objects are arranged. Child puts them back in order.

6. Have child make up stories about things and happenings around and tell them to other children.

7. Tell stories to a small group so that child feels he has your attention.

8. Show pictures of familiar scenes (e.g., mother washing dishes, a father painting a house, etc.). Tell the child about each one in a simple sentence.

9. First introduce words which represent concrete objects a child can see (e.g., ball, book), then action words the child can do (hit, touch, etc.). Later introduce words that can be represented

by pictures. Finally, abstract words and sentences may be learned. Use words suggested by children.

10. Have child group picture objects and tell why he grouped them in a particular way.

11. For a child whose speech is fast, slow, uneven, etc., use a tape recorder and play back his conversations, stories, etc. Discuss them with him.

12. If a child has trouble expressing himself in written work, have him plan a verbal report on his activities.

13. Children enjoy asking and answering riddles. This is a good activity for language development (e.g., "What am I?" I eat grass and give milk; I am made of leather, I have heels and soles, and you walk in me, etc.) .

14. Plan radio programs and present to class with the use of a microphone. Use tape recorders.

15. Charades. Act out phrases, sentences, ideas. Have child make up ideas to be acted out. Have another child try to guess what the group is acting out.

16. Have child dramatize literature, history, social studies, etc., so that he understands the meanings of new words in such contexts.

17. Say an object word. Have the child find a picture of it.

18. Say an action word. Have the child find a picture that portrays this action.

19. Word games. "I'm thinking of a word that tells you how you feel when you are hurt." Have the child give as many word answers as he can. Can be played in teams, keeping a tally of the number of words each team thinks of for each statement.

20. Talk about what *you* are doing when working on projects, etc. (e.g., naming materials, telling what the different children are doing, etc.) so that children hear your conversation.

21. Word family game. Assign the name of a word which is part of a family to each child (e.g., flowers, streets, people, etc.). Choose a child to be "it." When "it" calls a word family, two players having words from that group assigned to them must exchange places. "It" tries to take one of their places. Whoever has lost his place assumes the name of the player who is "it." After three tries, another player takes his place.

22. Have the child tell you the names of all the things he can see. Make a list for him so he can add more words.

23. Encourage the child to write get-well and thank-you cards. At first, let him draw a picture and let him tell you what to write.

24. To strengthen imagery, write words like *hot, cold, wet, bang, swish* on blackboard or paper. Have child draw or find picture of something related to each word and copy the word under the picture.

25. Teacher tells a story, children suggest what the ending must be.

26. Child reads a story, decides what pictures should be made. He then draws picture (roll of wallpaper, using the back, is suggested), telling the story in picture form. Cut hole in side of cardboard carton. Insert dowel through hollow center of roll. Insert paper in hole. Move picture by turning dowel so that you have a moving-picture story.

27. Have child keep a file of words he can read. Adding to the file is fun.

28. Treasure hunt. Obtain a supply of old magazines which the children can cut up. Develop a list of picturable statements (e.g., wash the clothes, smoke a cigarette, eat a candy bar). Divide the students into two teams. Place the cards face down on a table. Each student draws three or four cards and then hunts through a magazine to find illustrations. If he is unable to find one, he may draw it. When a child is finished with the first cards, he may obtain more.

29. The teacher makes several cards containing the names of objects in the room. He hands one to a child, who then places it next to the object.

30. Cards with directions on them are placed face down on a table. A child picks a card, reads it, places it face down again, and then follows the direction given (especially useful for safety directions).
Examples:

Drink some water	Go to sleep
Open the door	Put on your hat
Take off your coat	Walk slowly
Do not run, walk	Look both ways
Fly like a bird	Hop like a rabbit

If he gets it right he holds the card.

III. Activities for Improving Reading Skills

A. WORD ATTACK: Picture clues, perception of general configuration, etc.; recognition through unusual characteristics of the word; recognition through similarities and known words; context clues, phonetic analysis, structural analysis, syllabication, and use of glossary and dictionary.

1. Use Initial Teaching Alphabet to teach reading. It is an excellent approach for children who have no auditory discrimination problems.

2. Have the child trace the word printed or written large on a card, saying the word in syllables as he traces. Have child remove the card from sight and write the word from memory.

3. Make up sentences with words that stress one letter (e.g., Sister Susan sat on a small swing. Brother bought Bob a big book).

4. Make lists of rhyming words to help child learn new ones.

5. Cover a word with a card and remove the card slowly to the right so that the letters are exposed in proper sequence.

6. Underline the first letter in the word. Variations: underline the first letter using a crayon; write the first letter in a different color.

7. Select any number of teams. Give each team a root word (e.g., shame, approve, important, appear, probable, etc.). See how many words the players can make from these words by adding various prefixes and suffixes. Have them use each new word in a sentence.

8. When a child misses a word while reading aloud, present it to him on a card. Have him trace it with his finger and say it again. Then have him take the word and copy it, saying it as he copies it.

9. Word Lotto is the same as Number Lotto. Various forms can be used. Words with pictures, words with words, numbers and words. Cards should be made up by teacher, or some of the children (older or more capable) if the game is

used to help special problems. Commercial forms are available for practice and fun only.

    a. Make up list of words (pictures or numbers) that create problems.

    b. Have child make up slips of paper with one word on each.

    c. Make up sheets with 16 squares (may be 9 or 25).

    d. At random select words and write them on sheets. No one word can appear twice on one sheet.

10. Keep a list of the words each child misses. Print each such word on transparent paper. Have the child find the word that exactly matches his word. Words may appear in sentences or on a list.

11. Word cards. Children match words to phrase (e.g., farmer, one who farms; gardener, one who gardens; singer, one who sings).

12. Use large three-dimensional wooden letters. Have child form words with these.

13. Use pictures to help describe and learn a new word.

14. Prepare word cards and colored "frames" of the same size with the shape of the word cut out. Put several in one envelope. Have child match them. Have child guess word from frame.

15. To help a child recognize initial sounds, consonant blends in words, etc., set up sentences such as, The man with a funny face is a cl_____.

16. Prepare a set of cards with words with the same phonogram: pan, fan, man, can, etc. Prepare a poster with a list of riddles (e.g., My word is can. Change one letter and get something we use on a hot day—fan. Again change one letter and get

something we cook in—pan. The child looks for the correct word to answer the riddle, etc.) .

B. MOTIVATION

1. Have one child or several members of the class dictate a story to the teacher, who writes it on large newsprint. Have them copy it into readers they are making for themselves. In this way children feel the story is theirs.

2. Make a list of word pictures. Children make their own. Teacher makes a class list. The teacher writes down many bits of poetry and original word pictures as children say them. This encourages children to listen for unusual and poetic words and phrases and make their own word pictures (e.g., the blue sky, the cool shade, etc.) .

3. Have child make up a riddle whose answer begins with the last letter of the answer to the previous riddle. (E.g., I say Bow-wow—dog; I am full of flowers—garden; Birds live in me—nests; garden begins with the last letter in dog, nests begins with the last letter in garden.)

4. Ask children if they would like to make up their own word or picture dictionary.

C. FLUENCY: Rhythm reading, meaningful phrasing, punctuation observed, adequate eye-voice span, phrase rather than word-by-word reading.

1. When a child moves his lips or sub-vocalizes as he reads silently, he reads slowly. Use a tachistoscope or a speed reader to encourage him to speed up so he cannot sub-vocalize. Make him conscious of his slow reading. Increase his eye span by using a card cut-out.

2. Choose a story in which the children can see marked differences in the persons or animals

speaking. "The Three Bears" gives contrast in the bear family. Have the children listen to the dialogue in such old tales as "Jack and the Bean-stalk" or "The Old Woman and the Fox." Encourage the children to show meaning and character as they read and get the audience reaction to the way the conversations are read.

3. Make a tape recording of the child's reading. Play it back immediately and have child evaluate and try to improve it.

4. Use a tachistoscope to encourage phrase reading. While it is good to start with a single word, the teacher must soon move to two-, three- and four-word phrases. Increasing the span of words a child sees is a matter of practice and habit formation.

5. Provide a good model for the child to imitate. Read a sentence orally with somewhat exaggerated phrasing, and then have the child imitate your reading the sentence. Reading of alternate sentences by teacher and child is also helpful. Some children gain considerable benefit from reading in unison with teacher.

D. COMPREHENSION: Concepts, imagination, insights; analytical skills; interpretive and critical skills.

1. Newspaper study: Find conflicting points of view. Have students evaluate them.

2. Name the story: Read short, simple stories to the group and have them make up a title for each story. The stories should be unfamiliar. Appropriate stories for this activity will often be found in readers or short story collections that are not regularly used by the group.

3. Have child find details in a picture that tell what might happen next (e.g., a tree almost ready to fall, a boy looking out the window at snow, a boy and a dog, two boys with fishing poles, two girls with jumping ropes, etc.) .

4. Assign a short selection for silent reading. Print a list of phrases or short sentences on the board, and have children choose those which contain the ideas in the selection.

5. Use written and oral absurdities, ridiculous statements mixed with true statements, to encourage critical thinking about what is being read.

6. When reading a story, stop occasionally to ask, "What will happen next?" Comprehension is necessary to realistic prediction.

7. Ask for the reason something happened during the reading of a selection.

8. Telling back: It is helpful to read a story to a group of slow readers and have them tell it back to you. At first, read it in short parts, later the entire story may be read. Write what they say on the chalkboard. They are helped by seeing the story written at their own vocabulary level. If a story is a particular favorite, it may be recorded more permanently on a chart or in a "big book," in which case one member of the group may occasionally read the simple version while the rest listen so they can tell the story later in their own words.

9. To reinforce, recall of details in sequence, the teacher lists significant statements or phrases about a story in random order. The children are asked to read the assigned selection and to find the statement that goes with each paragraph.

10. Summarize a story: The teacher reads a short story to the group and has the pupils retell the plot in one sentence. Children may need considerable help in making a good summary. Use stories which are on the reading level of the group. At first, give them several examples of a short summary and help them decide which is the best.

11. Let the child make up experience stories in his own words. Instead of reading about children who may be quite different from him, living in an unfamiliar type of environment, and doing things that he has never done, he should explore experiences about himself and his classmates in his own language. By doing this, the reading matter is sure to be phrased in language that is natural to him and to be vitally interesting because he has helped to write it.

12. Find the sentence for the picture: Cut out some small, attractive pictures from magazines or old books. Prepare a set of cards with one sentence on each card. Each sentence should describe one of the pictures. Put the pictures and sentences in an envelope or box. The child matches the sentence to the picture.

13. The children blindfold their eyes while the teacher hides cards in different places about the room. One child is chosen to search for a card. When he finds one he reads it silently, then acts it out while the rest of the class guesses what his card says (e.g., close the window, hop like a bunny, etc.). The pupil who guesses correctly is then given an opportunity to search for a card and dramatize it. When all cards have been

found, some pupils may be selected to hide them again.

14. Have the children read a story. Have sentences which relate to sequence of events in story written on cards. Have the children put them in order.

15. Make-believe or true? Discuss the difference between true stories and stories in which imaginary events take place. Then give an example of a very short story of each type. One or two sentences will do. Then ask children to tell which story is make-believe and which is true. When the children are familiar with the difference between the two types, a child may volunteer to tell a story. The story may be of some imaginary event or of something which could really happen. The storyteller then asks another child, "Make-believe or true?" (E.g., "The Cow Jumped Over the Moon" and "The cow gave some good milk for supper," etc.) .

E. PRACTICE

1. When a child reads wrong words, pick them out. Give him a paragraph to read with wrong words or phrases underlined. Tell him the correct word. Have him practice the word in any way he wants to (e.g., draw a picture, write it, etc.) . Have two children work together.

2. Playing postman: Collect a set of 3 x 5″ cards with words that need to be practiced. A large cereal box that has been decorated gaily makes a good mailbox. Cut a hole 3½ x 4″ wide near the top of one side. Construct another box the same way and place the two side by side. Label one "Mailbox" and the other "Dead Letters."

The children draw cards in turn. If a child knows the word on his card, he may mail it; otherwise, he is told the word and the card goes into the "Dead Letter" box. Child strives to mail all of his cards as letters.

3. Peg it: A pegboard with three or four pegs, one for each player, may be used for this game. Prepare three or four sets of word cards and punch a hole in a corner of each card. The dealer gives an equal number of cards to each player. In turn, each player draws three cards from his own pile and reads them. Each card that he reads correctly may be hung on his peg; if read incorrectly, he is told the correct word and the card must be discarded. The player with the most cards on his peg wins.

4. Dominoes: Prepare a series of small rectangular cards in the shape of dominoes with words in the place of the dots. Follow the rules of Dominoes. This game may also be played with phrases.

5. "I Am Wishing": Label a shoebox with the words "Toy Chest." Assemble a set of cards with "toy words" on them (e.g., airplanes, ball, bicycle, blocks, boat, bunny, cars, engine, hammer, scooter). Each player has about three cards, and the leader holds the Toy Chest. The leader calls for a toy by saying, "I am wishing for a *ball*." The player who has the corresponding word says, "I can make your wish come true." He reads his card aloud, then puts it away in the box.

6. We take a trip: Draw a diagram of a long path on the blackboard or on a heavy piece of cardboard. At the end of this path draw a schoolhouse, barn, zoo, etc. Along the path write short sentences for moving ahead toward the schoolhouse. The child

who reads his words or phrases or sentences correctly may carry out the directions, otherwise he is told what they say and he stays in place. The child who reaches his destination first wins.

7. Divide the class into teams. Give each child a word card. Teacher says a sentence. Each child runs to make the sentence with his group. The group that makes the sentence first gets a point.

F. Accuracy: Mispronunciation, repetitions, omissions, additions, hesitations, reversals, refusals, left-to-right reading.

1. Have child trace a problem with his finger so that he becomes aware of any omission, additions or reversals.

2. If a child mispronounces a sound in one word, ask him to say another word which will help him form the sound correctly.

3. Have the child read easy material aloud. He should not be asked to read difficult material to the group. Hesitations and refusals are sometimes the result of fear of being embarrassed.

4. If child tends to leave out a particular part of a word or certain words, rewrite the sentence using a color for the word or underlining the part in color.

5. Provide positive approval when a child corrects an error he has been making.

IV. Activities for Improving Skills in Mathematics

A. Numeration, Counting and Number Concepts

1. Give kinesthetic reinforcement to counting. Have child count while he claps, taps or jumps.

2. Use regular playing cards. Have child put the hearts, spades, etc., in order.

3. Have child hop on numbers drawn on the floor or pavement in sequence and ask him to call each number as he hops.

4. Have child use number combinations throughout the day in any experience that suggests it (e.g., taking attendance, counting milk or lunch orders, handling milk money, bank money, passing papers, materials, etc.). Do not let it become a chore. Vary the activity. Make sure the child who needs this practice tells you what he is doing so you know he understands the activity. Frequently, it has no meaning at all to him.

5. Write a series of numbers on the chalkboard. Erase them one by one and say them.

6. Have child practice walking backward, counting backward as he moves. First put numbers on board.

7. A guessing game: Cards with numbers are arranged in sequence. Have one child close his eyes; another removes a card. "It" must name the missing number.

8. On walks, have child read numbers on houses, license plates, prices in stores, etc.

B. NON-NUMERICAL CONCEPTS

1. Play games involving a child's being "out" for a short time. Say "Whoever misses the ball is 'out' —how many are left?" (E.g., musical chairs, farmer in the dell.)

2. Have child pile up blocks of several sizes, placing the largest at the bottom.

3. Have children cut strips of paper. Instruct them to cut them short, long, narrow, wide, etc.

4. Play "Simon Says," giving instructions to move over, under, behind, on top of, in front of, forward, backward, in the middle, etc.

C. PLACE VALUE
1. Put all ones in squares and all tens in circles until child learns place of each.
2. Make all ones one color and tens another. Be consistent until the child learns the task.

D. PROCESSES OR COMBINATIONS OF PROCESSES
1. Use *real* money to teach the basic facts. Use it as the child plays store, or just imagines he is buying things. Often a child can learn with money what he can't learn any other way.
2. Have the child verbalize as he relates number sequence and facts.
3. Have child verbalize steps in arithmetic as he does his practice work.
4. Have child bring in large numbers found in newspapers. Compare, read, tell values.
5. Have children play card games, using commercial playing cards, counting the hearts or spades and saying the number. Play "Fish," "Old Maid" or any other simple game.
6. Have child make a slide-rule, a rulerlike card with digits on it up to 20. The second card or ruler is in a different color. Slide the first rule along the top of the background numbers, until it exposes one number to be added (e.g., 4 is exposed in top rule. The number on the bottom rule is added. The answer appears on the top rule over the number added).

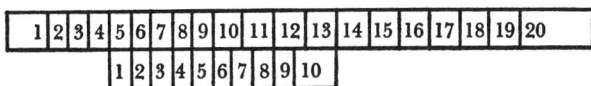

1	2	3	4	5	6	7	8	9	10	11	12	13	14	15	16	17	18	19	20
		1	2	3	4	5	6	7	8	9	10								

Child may see that $4 + 2 = 6$; $4 + 5 = 9$, etc. Instruct him to slide it along to show that $6 + 7 = 13$, etc.

7. Use bean bags to throw on numbers drawn on the floor or playground. Have child keep score.
8. Make puzzle cards of combinations with answers. Have child fit together. Make sure only the right answer will fit.

9. Play a game. Have two teams. Assign a number to each child. Give each child a large card with his number on it. Put an answer (10) on the chalkboard. Call on #4 to stand. Ask for his partner to join him to make 10, etc. Have them line up with their numbers in front.
10. Have child make individual fact cards for himself with the answer on back. Child may teach himself by making a pile of the ones he gets wrong and a pile of the ones he gets right.
11. Tap out combinations of numbers. Child taps out answers.

E. FRACTIONS

1. Without calling them fractions, use them in everyday situations. Ask child to bring you a half or a fourth of something (a quarter of a dollar), so these words become part of vocabulary before fractions are introduced as an expanding concept. Make sure you involve parts of whole things and parts of groups.
2. Use real objects such as money, groups of children, pies, etc., when introducing fractions to children who may have trouble with the concept

Later, representational materials will serve (e.g., cardboard cutouts, buttons, etc.) .

F. MONEY

1. Bring in menus from restaurants around town, or make some up. Have child order a meal and pay for it. Use this to teach giving change.

2. Teach additive method for making change as store clerks do (e.g., have one dollar, spent 57 cents, 3 pennies makes 60, one dime and a nickel make 75 and a quarter makes one dollar.) Use real money whenever the opportunity presents itself.

3. Play musical chairs but make each chair worth a sum of money. Whoever sits on the chair gets the money. In order to keep it, the child must tell you how much he has altogether (adding all previous times) .

4. Play money games. Make color charts on bulletin board or blackboard with amounts of money written in squares on the chart. Count by 5s, 10s, 25s, etc. Shoot guns with rubber darts and have cashier pay the student who shoots the gun whatever amount of money the dart lands on. Make change to get the right amount of money. The one who has the most money after everyone has had a turn is the winner, and he gets to be the cashier next time.

5. Have a classroom store and let each child play store by buying and selling articles, paying for them and making change. Use real money so child can identify actual coins.

6. Have each child take a turn selling hot lunch tickets, collecting bank books in the room or participating in other money handling activities.

G. Time

1. Discuss the importance of being on time for jobs, meals, appointments, etc., and the relationship of these factors to other people's responsibilities.

2. Write a particular time on paper. When clock in room shows that time, child should notify teacher.

3. Set up model clock in classroom. Show relationship between printed time (10:00, for example) and time as it appears on the face of a clock.

4. Obtain used time clock. Have child punch cards at various times to get time sense. Help him measure the amount of time it takes for him to complete certain tasks. Do not overwhelm him with time so that serious anxiety is evoked.

5. Make clocks picturing things that happen at different times of the day (e.g., waking up—picture of alarm clock ringing or person getting out of bed).

6. Have a set of cards with clocks on them. Show child one card, have him copy time on his blank clock. Discuss what time it is.

7. Midnight Matching Clock Card Game. Make a set of cards with each card having a clockface, minute and hour hands showing a particular time, and the time marked below the clockface. Make a duplicate set of cards leaving out the marked time below the clockface (e.g., 8:10). Each player is given 8 or 10 *unmarked* cards. Leader holds up a marked card. Children with matching cards turn the card over. When all cards are turned over, children call out, "Midnight." Check by reading back the times from

the winner's cards and checking with the leader's cards.

8. Have children bring in TV and radio schedules. Ask them to show on a clock when certain programs begin and end, how long they run, etc.

9. Discuss what happens on different days of the week. Put days on board. Put pictures of what happens next to days and times of the day.

H. SYSTEMS OF MEASUREMENT

1. Have charts on display that show comparison of different measures to be used for reference, showing real relation of smaller measure to larger (e.g., distance, time, weight).

2. Have child fill different size cartons and containers with water. Set up comparisons. Have child write what he has found (e.g., pint, quart, gallon, etc.).

3. Have child plan and carry out activities which involve measurement. Use sewing, cooking and hobbies, etc.

4. Give child a list of items to buy. Ask him to list three different sizes of the same item and their cost.

5. If child does not know quantity (pints, quarts, half-gallon, gallon, pound, one-half pound, dozen, one-half dozen), set up a store having empty cartons of different sizes. Give child a list, including various quantities of items which he must purchase. Have him select right containers. Then have him list what he has bought.

6. Obtain a scale. Weigh some common objects. Show how one object might weigh the same as two of another object. Note actual weights.

7. Play a game. Have children pick up objects and guess approximate weights. The one who is closest receives 5 points, next 3 points, etc.

8. Have child weigh different objects and write labels of weight to display on them.

9. Play oral and written games which ask child to estimate size, weight, cost, distance, time. Have him compare his answers with real answers to see how close he gets. Teams or individuals.

10. Plan and take a trip. Use transportation schedules to plan it. Follow schedules. Discuss the words.

11. Have children make up their own schedules. Tell children what time "A" train leaves and arrives, "B" train, etc.

12. Explain actual bus and train schedules. Ask children questions orally. Have children tell which train, etc., will be first.

V. Activities for Improving Behavior skills

A. CREATING A HEALTHY LEARNING ENVIRONMENT

1. Have child choose a project which helps someone else (e.g., teach safety rules to younger child, teach how to take care of a pet, do a show for older people, collect for a cause). Have him plan and carry out entire enterprise with teacher acting as resource consultant.

2. A large mouth or ears could be placed on the bulletin board with a box attached. Rather than tattling aloud, children must write reports and put them in the box. At the end of the day these are removed and read aloud to emphasize how silly most of them are when cold. This should be a meaningful evaluation.

3. Permit child to schedule the day after agreeing on the work to be done. Periodically evaluate with individuals, small groups, and entire class to broaden understanding for planning and increase meaning of independent activity.

4. Develop a working behavior code for the classroom. Indicate that the child will develop one rule at a time, test and evaluate it, then make a decision concerning its adoption. State that the only limitation occurs when the rule is detrimental to the best interests of a child or involves a school rule, law or safety code. Indicate clearly that the decision of the class will stand. (Carry this out or the value of the experience is lost.)

5. Set up class government. Authority to govern must be real and spelled out to avoid mockery. The more authority you can yield to the children the better; however, any amount of authority is good as long as it is clearly defined and understood.

6. Always introduce new materials in conjunction with old material so that the child feels the security of relating it to what he knows.

B. FEELINGS ABOUT SELF

1. If a student cannot accept responsibilities for errors, is a poor sport, etc., work individually on problems to improve his skills in specific areas so he becomes more proficient (e.g., ball catching, memory, running, etc.) .

2. Give youngsters minimal authority positions and establish a system of reporting the completion and success of tasks (e.g., delivered a message, answered the phone, etc.) .

3. The tease and bully is asking for attention because of his feelings of inadequacy or because this is the behavior he has been taught. It is important to give him extra time and attention when he is quiet to help him develop special interests which improve his self-confidence.

4. If child does not make friends easily, pair him with another child having the same interests.

5. Have pupils draw and talk about situations which make them *angry*. Then list specific things they can do to "cool off." The children should make the suggestions.

6. If a child has trouble expressing himself, have him tell what he did at recess or lunchtime as soon as he returns to school, while his memory is still fresh and when the task is simple.

7. Encourage the child with a problem of expressing himself verbally to write about an activity which has just taken place. Have him attempt to verbalize what he is writing in the diary.

8. Have a discussion with child. Try to help him discover ways in which he might help another child and provide the opportunity for this to happen.

9. During discussions of feelings, have children pantomime sadness, happiness, etc., for better understanding.

10. Promote child-initiated discussions of how children feel in various situations. Set aside a time when the group may discuss any phase of their feelings and emotions.

11. When a child shows positive behavior and control and finds acceptable outlets for aggressiveness, heap praise upon him and let rest of class know about it.

12. When a child becomes angry, attempt to put the child's feelings into words when the situation occurs (e.g., "You feel angry when you cannot have a toy."). Ask the child, "What is it you want to say?" Personalize aggressive behavior (e.g., "How would you feel if Jimmy pushed you, took your toy," etc.).

13. Have children write or dictate stories about themselves. Some topics may be: When I Grow Up, What I Like to Do Most, My Favorite Experience, Something I'd Like to Have.

14. Let the child keep lists of the problems he has overcome and work he has successfully completed so that he can see his progress easily.

15. Have the student make a list of things that make him important. Have him develop areas if there are few. (E.g., caring for someone, doing a job well, helping someone in need of help, being a good friend, etc.)

16. If he feels left out and worthless, have the student become responsible for something the class thinks is important.

17. Have the disadvantaged student find individuals who have been successful despite having come from the same background as his own.

18. Make sure the student works at tasks that he can successfully complete. Only the worst kind of human being destroys a student by forcing him to work at tasks he cannot possibly perform successfully.

19. Try a game you might call "Turtle." Develop the idea that sometimes the best course of action is to pretend you don't hear if others are teasing you. Only students who do not think much of themselves tease others.

20. Plan activities that will let each child's strong points come out (e.g., singing, drawing, a special collection, etc.).

21. Hang a full-length mirror in the classroom and post questions beside the mirror so each student can check himself on hair, hemline, neatness, colors, and other points the class decides are important to a good appearance.

22. When a child is young, below eleven years old, a conference which helps parents understand the importance of being neat may be helpful. When the child becomes older, his lack of cleanliness may be a reaction against the parental pressure to be neat. A conference to help relieve this pressure may help.

23. Involve the child in projects which give him an opportunity to care for his own clothes (e.g., working the washing machine, cleaning them, sewing on a button, ironing them).

24. Help the child develop a self-evaluation checklist. Indicate growth as child learns new things. Help the child look at his strengths and weaknesses in relation to the tasks demanded of him in school and in work in the future.

25. Pair a popular member of the class with a child who has trouble being accepted. Explain to the popular member the importance of his role and help him evaluate how successful he is. *Do not use pressure,* since the loss may be greater than the gain.

26. Meet with each student privately at least weekly. Discuss his progress. Help him work out possible goals for the coming few days. Reward meaningfully and appropriately for previous success.

27. Ask a child to be the special friend of a child with a problem. Help both evaluate the relationship.

28. Find an area where the child can perform better than a classmate or find a child in another room he can help. Make this an important, advertised activity.

29. Plan an activity for the child which gives him an opportunity to demonstrate what he has accomplished in a particular area of interest (e.g., visit by parent, exhibits which are shown to other classes, invitations to other outside visitors).

30. Observe difficult child's behavior. Acknowledge each positive act loudly and clearly to the class and to others in the school. When behavior is negative, try to ignore it and try to help other children ignore it. When behavior cannot be ignored, try to control the child with the least amount of attention possible. Speak softly, control quickly.

31. Have student take responsibility for helping a younger child with the same or similar problem to his. Help him evaluate his behavior and develop insights.

32. If student is not otherwise motivated or feels negatively about himself, develop a reward system as an incentive to learn. This may be permission to play a game, work on his project, have a candy, etc. Gradually remove the external incentives to build internal incentive system.

33. At appropriate times praise each student's efforts on a personal, one-to-one basis. If you do not feel you can praise, you probably cannot help that student.

34. Ask child to choose task for which he will act independently and be responsible (e.g., collecting money for trips, suggesting how a game might be organized, a book for a report); reward the behavior appropriately.

35. Show affection and positive attention for the child who will not respond initially. Do not punish for lack of reaction. It will take a long time to get responses even under the best conditions.

36. Teach a game or give directions for doing something to one child—something the child and the class want to do. Then have the child teach or explain to the class.

37. Stop and talk game. Players form a double circle and walk around each other. At the signal each two standing side by side must start talking about an announced topic (e.g., favorite TV program, favorite sport). Continue to show how easy it is to talk and carry on a conversation.

38. Use a self-rating character chart (see page 51). Discuss with child frequently.

C. RELATIONSHIPS WITH OTHERS: Relates to problems such as indications of negative relationships; rejected by others in games; hurts other children; gets others into trouble; lack of friends; is not thoughtful.

1. Have youngster compile a list of the reasons he is in conflict with his peers. Help him choose one or more of these reasons to concentrate upon weekly. Have him evaluate the success of his efforts and compare these with the opinions of other members of his peer group. (Be prepared to arbitrate objectively in some cases.)

2. If a child teases or bullies, pair him with a child who is the butt of many jokes. Explain the responsibility of each child.

3. When child commits an act which is a nuisance or hurts others, set up a round-table group to discuss actions of this nature and the reactions of the group. Offender should be part of the group discussion and perhaps will gain insight into his behavior, if he can be kept from being defensive.

4. Make things such as cards, books, crafts to send to people who are ill or handicapped. Discuss these sharing activities.

5. If child finds it difficult to share, share some of your possessions with him—a favorite book, poem, rock or shell collection, paints, etc. Discuss this with him.

6. Provide opportunities for the children to share their homemade products with the class, such as a sharing period or display table with each *child* putting his name on his product.

7. Plan for pairs of children to color together sharing one box of crayons. Discuss the need to wait one's turn to use a color being used by the partner, and to use another color until that desired color is available.

8. Plan specific group activities such as a show, party, demonstration, etc., where each child has a specific important role. Do several if there are large numbers of children. Have children evaluate as they plan and carry out their roles in relation to others.

9. Have children suggest activities. Choose those where success depends upon the cooperation of

the members of the group. Help class to analyze the interdependent needs of the members.

10. Divide group into competitive teams and give them problems that must be solved by the team within a specific time, including bonus points for full completion before time expires. Rotate team captains, allowing each team member a turn to be in command and decide how to attack problems (e.g., best way to run safety campaign, best way to set up good bulletin board display, how to decide what to purchase for a party, best way to distribute papers, etc., depending on age level of children). Try methods children suggest to show which will work out best. Make reward tangible.

11. Have two children put a puzzle together. Make it important that they help each other. Have several teams compete to make a contest out of it.

12. Write notes to parents telling of a play, art show, music day, or other school activity. Children can decide what should be said and with teacher's help this can be put on the blackboard for everyone to copy.

D. INDIVIDUAL RELATIONSHIPS TO ENVIRONMENT: Relates to problems in these areas: values, obligations, rules, stealing, lack of responsibility, lies, distortion, gambling, dislike of school, lack of initiative, inability to function independently, drawing conclusions without thinking through, etc.

1. If a young child appears to tell untrue stories, he may not know the difference between the truth and the things he imagines. Help him by discussing the difference with him and ask him to

tell you which things he says he thinks are true and which are imagined.

2. If child does not clean up his materials, permit him to take only one article at a time and see that he puts it back before he takes another. Have each child be responsible for toys he takes out. Encourage others who have played with them to help.

3. If child is prone to steal, make him responsible for keeping track of a piece of class equipment. Praise him for the good job he is doing.

4. If child takes things that belong to others, he may not have learned the concept of ownership. Label all things around the classroom and help him learn which are his, which belong to others, and which belong to the class as a whole.

5. Reward all children who find objects in classroom and return them immediately.

6. For the child who has trouble finding things to do to occupy his leisure time, and thus finds trouble, have a wide variety of ideas available. Help him develop a hobby or interest that he can keep up for some time.

7. If child talks out of turn continually, create situations where he is in a small group and has ample opportunity to hold forth.

8. When a student is not prompt, try to help him find activities or chores he wants to do and will enjoy. Help him be prompt in order to succeed in these activities (e.g., safety patrol, classroom helper, cafeteria helper, etc.). This will work most successfully if financial or other desired awards are present.

9. Have child act as a big brother to a new child. His task is to integrate youngster into group and help the child learn and follow group rules.

10. Have child draw pictures about positive acts of social behavior such as opening a door for a person carrying bundles, getting into line, raising hand in classroom. A simple movie can be made with these pictures and the behavior can be reviewed by showing these pictures. A diorama using pipecleaner figures showing these considerate acts can be made.

11. Play games which involve taking turns—pitching horseshoes, basketball, baseball, "King and Queen," "Hide the Eraser." Emphasize the rules relating to taking turns.

12. If a child does not follow the rules in regard to discussion, be careful to call on the child for answers as often as you call on others. Do not interrupt children when they are speaking. Give verbal emphasis to this practice by saying, "Is there anything else you would like to say before it's John's turn?" Use the tape recorder, since only one person can use the microphone at once.

13. If children use unacceptable language and talk out, have them organize an informal club, possibly more than one, providing a social setting within the classroom in which attention is paid to the manners of speaking in a situation which would ordinarily condone slang if it occurred outside the classroom. (Type of club would depend on age and interests of children.)

14. When the child does not seem to be aware of the use of courteous formal expressions (i.e., thank you, please, you are welcome, apology, greeting, offering) , the teacher must use these expressions

and give verbal recognition and reinforcement to other children's use of such expressions.

15. Make a floor plan of the school and mark in red the places, and list practices, the child recognizes as potentially dangerous.

16. Collect a series of pictures and have students find something in them which might be a dangerous practice. Have class members list as many accidents as they can think of that could happen in such situations.

17. Have children plan a dramatization such as a class television program which reviews safety rules in dramatic form.

18. Have children make class notebooks about home and school accidents and how they can be avoided. Include pictures, safety rules, common dangers in the home and school and all things discussed in class. Record accidents as they happen and note why they occurred.

19. Have the school nurse teach students simple first aid rules and help them learn about safe procedures in school.

20. Have each child choose a table at which to sit in the cafeteria. He is to observe how other children act, the effect of this behavior on the others, and on the entire group. Observations are the basis for discussion and understanding of the need of self-control. This activity can be used to evaluate behavior in other situations.

21. Have children write a dictionary of "hip" language.

22. Have children choose a topic to discuss or debate which has several possible positions. Encourage a variety of opinions and those who hold an independent point of view whether it is right or

wrong. (Later, when the students have built independent behavior, the teacher can point out errors.)

23. Select activities of high interest which require using knowledge acquired in new ways (e.g., "what if" games which deal with real situations such as these: You are babysitting and the baby becomes ill? There is a fire in your house and you are the first to notice it? You are camping and a member of your group is missing? You are in a car on a remote road and have car trouble you cannot repair?). This game can be changed to meet whatever rules or situations the teacher wishes to emphasize.

24. Have children prepare a class newspaper with different opinions on an issue. Students are responsible for running it.

25. During the early stages of decision-making, permit children to choose between two possibilities only—two toys, two places to go, two things to do, etc. Discuss the reasons for making choices. As children are successful, increase the number of choices. The goal is to help children learn to operate independently.

26. Have small groups make up a class schedule and present it to the class. Children must explain why they have chosen this schedule. Rotate this responsibility. If schedule is not impossible, have the class carry it out and then evaluate its success and reasons for their decision.

27. Encourage discussions of free-time activity both in and out of school. Make up a list. Help children learn how to evaluate their choices by asking questions (e.g., Is the activity appropriate for the weather, the number of people

involved, the place, the funds available, time and skills required, equipment needs?).

28. If a child cannot think of what he would like to write, ask him to think of what he would like to know about a friend and write this information. Suggest a weekly log.

29. If a child cannot remember how to write a letter, give him a simple outline of letter form to keep as a model and to copy from.

Bibliography

Bettelheim, Bruno, "Teaching the Disadvantaged." *NEA Journal,* September 1965.

———, "The Decision to Fail." *The School Review,* Vol. 69, Winter 1961.

Bloom, Benjamin, *Stability and Change in Human Characteristics.* New York, John Wiley & Sons, 1964.

Bower, Eli M., "The Emotionally Handicapped Child and the School." *Journal of Exceptional Children,* September 1959.

———, Tashnovian, P. J., and Larson, C. A., *A Process for Early Identification of Emotionally Disturbed Children.* Sacramento, California State Department of Education, 1959.

Bradford, L. P., Gibb, J. R., and Benne, K. D., eds., *T-Group Theory and Laboratory Methods: Innovation in Re-Education.* New York, John Wiley & Sons, 1964.

Buch, Herbert, "Theoretical Aspects of Psychological Behavior in the Brain Damaged." *Psychological Services for the Cerebral Palsied,* Morton Goldstein, United Cerebral Palsy Association, 1956.

Chesler, Mark, and Fox, Robert, "Role Playing Methods in the Classroom," Chicago Science Research Associates, 1966.

Cronbach, Lee, *Essentials of Psychological Testing.* New York, Harper Brothers., 1949.

Cruickshank, William and Johnson, Orville, *Psychology of Exceptional Children and Youth.* Englewood Cliffs, N.J., Prentice-Hall, 1958.

Delp, Harold A., *The Training School Bulletin,* 52:9, January 1956.

Freidus, Elizabeth, "Methodology for the Classroom Teacher." *The Special Child in Century 21,* Jerome Hellmuth, ed. Published in Seattle, Washington, by The Special Child Publications, 1964.

Gallagher, James M., and Moss, James W., "New Concepts of Intelligence and Their Effects on Exceptional Children." *Exceptional Children,* September, 1963.

Goodenough, Florence L., *Exceptional Children.* New York, Appleton-Century-Crofts, Inc., 1956.

Gorman, Mike, *Every Other Bed.* New York, World Publishing Co., 1956.

Guilford, J. P., "The Structure of Intellect." *Psychological Bulletin,* 1956.

Havighurst, Robert J., *Development Tasks and Education,* 2nd ed. New York, Longmans, Green and Co., 1952.

Hunt, J. McV., *Intelligence and Experience.* New York, Ronald Press, 1961.

Johnson, Arthur C., Jr., "Our Schools Make Criminals." *Journal of Criminal Law and Criminology,* XXXIII, No. 4 November–December, 1942) , 310–12 (reprinted by special permission from the *Journal of Criminal Law and Criminology* (Northwestern University School of Law) .

Johnson, Orville G., "Guidance for Exceptional Children," in Cruickshank, William M., and Johnson, Orville G., *Exceptional Children and Youth.* Englewood Cliffs, N.J., Prentice-Hall, 1958.

Kephart, Newell C., *The Slow Learner in the Classroom.* Columbus, Ohio, Charles E. Merrill Books, Inc., 1960.

Kirk, Samuel, *Educating Exceptional Children.* Boston, Houghton Mifflin Co., 1962.

Kuhlen, Raymond G., *The Psychology of Adolescent Development.* New York, Harper & Brothers, 1952.

Lippit, Ronald, "Understanding Classroom Social Relations and Learning." Chicago Science Research Associates, 1966.

Magnuson, Henry W., and others, "Evaluating Pupil Progress." California State Department of Education, Vol. XXI, No. 6, April 1952, The Department, Sacramento.

Mallison, Ruth, "Individual Educational Therapy for the Special Child," in *The Special Child in Century 21,* Jerome Hellmuth, ed. Special Child Publication of the Segrum School, Inc., 1964.

Quillen, L. James, and Hanna, Lavonne A., *Education for Social Competence.* New York, Scott, Foresman & Co., 1948.

Reynolds, M.D., "A Framework for Considering Some Issues in Special Education." *Exceptional Children,* March 1962.

Santa Barbara County Program of Evaluation: Developing Concepts, Attitudes, and Skills, Vol. 8. Prepared under the direction of the Office of the County Superintendent of Schools, Santa Barbara County, Santa Barbara, California: Schauer Printing Studio, Inc., 1945.

Sarason, Seymour B., *Psychological Problems in Mental Deficiency.* Harper & Brothers, New York, 1949.

"Self-Rating Character Chart." Los Angeles Public Schools, 1949, in *Evaluating Pupil Progress,* Magnuson, Henry W., and others. California State Department of Education, Sacramento, Vol. XXI, No. 6, April 1952.

Sociometry in Group Relations. American Council on Education, Washington, D.C., 1948.

Stratemeyer, Florence B., and others, *Developing a Curriculum for Modern Living,* 2nd ed. New York, Bureau of Publications, Teachers College, Columbia University, 1957.

The United Cerebral Palsy Research and Educational Foundation. *Program for Calendar Year 1958.* New York, The Foundation, 1958.

Wortis, Joseph, "A Note on the Concept of the Brain Injured Child." *American Journal on Mental Deficiency,* 61:204–206, 1956.

Watson, Goodwin, "What Do We Know About Learning?" *National Education Association Journal,* March 1963.

Wiles, Kimball, *Teaching for Better Schools.* Englewood Cliffs, N.J., Prentice-Hall, 1959.

Young, Milton, "Planning Programs for the Disadvantaged." *Connecticut Teacher,* Connecticut Education Association, March 1966.

The following are additional references:

Bond, G. L., and Tinker, M. A., *Reading Difficulties: Their Diagnosis and Correction.* New York, Appleton-Century-Crofts, 1957.

Brueckner, L. J., and Bond, G. L., *The Diagnosis and Treatment of Learning Difficulties.* New York, Appleton-Century-Crofts, 1955.

DeVault, M. V., *Improving Mathematics Programs: Trends and Issues in the Elementary School.* Columbus, Ohio, Charles E. Merrill Books, 1961.

Dinkmeyer, D., and Dreikurs, D., *Encouraging Children to Learn: the Encouragement Process.* Englewood Cliffs, N.J., Prentice-Hall, 1963.

Durrell, D. D., *Teaching Young Children to Read.* Conference proceedings ed. by Warren G. Cutts. Washington, D.C., U.S. Department of Health, Education, and Welfare, 1964.

Figarel, A. J., ed., *Changing Concepts of Reading Instruction.* International Reading Association Conference Proceedings, Vol. 6. New York, Scholastic Magazines, 1961.

Freeman, F. N., *Teaching Handwriting.* Bulletin No. 4. *What Research Says to the Teacher.* Washington, D.C., National Education Association, 1954.

Grossnickle, F. E., and Brueckner, L. J., *Discovering Meanings in Elementary School Mathematics,* 4th ed. New York, Holt, Rinehart and Winston, 1963.

Kephart, N. C., *The Slow Learner in the Classroom.* Columbus, Ohio, Charles E. Merrill Books, 1960.

Kirk, S. A., and McCarthy, J. J., "The Illinois Test of Psycholinguistic Abilities—An Approach to Differential Diagnosis." *American Journal of Mental Deficiency,* 66: 1961.

Maslow, A. H., *Toward a Psychology of Being.* Princeton, N.J., Van Nostrand, 1962.

Otto, Wayne, and McMenemy, Richard A., *Corrective and Remedial Teaching: Principles and Practices.* Boston, Houghton Mifflin, 1966.

Rogers, C. R., *On Becoming a Person.* Boston, Houghton Mifflin, 1961.

Index